PAID IN FULL

TALES OF BRAVERY & SACRIFICE

KEN BYERLY

CONTENTS

This moving drawing was completed by Linda Stoeffler, wife of John R. Stoeffler, PMC, Class of '63 and author of the poem A Bad Day At Bong Son (RVN).

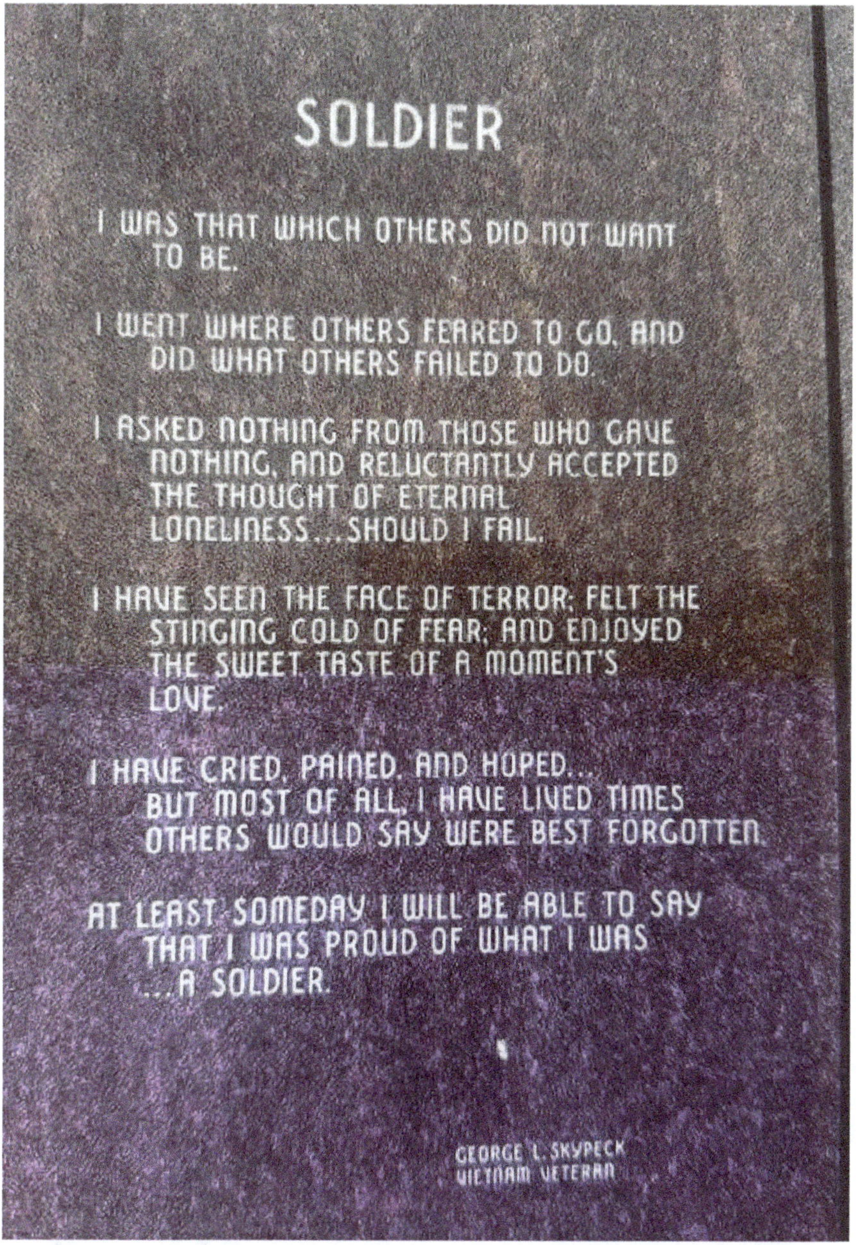

SOLDIER

I WAS THAT WHICH OTHERS DID NOT WANT
TO BE.

I WENT WHERE OTHERS FEARED TO GO, AND
DID WHAT OTHERS FAILED TO DO.

I ASKED NOTHING FROM THOSE WHO GAVE
NOTHING, AND RELUCTANTLY ACCEPTED
THE THOUGHT OF ETERNAL
LONELINESS...SHOULD I FAIL.

I HAVE SEEN THE FACE OF TERROR; FELT THE
STINGING COLD OF FEAR; AND ENJOYED
THE SWEET TASTE OF A MOMENT'S
LOVE.

I HAVE CRIED, PAINED, AND HOPED...
BUT MOST OF ALL, I HAVE LIVED TIMES
OTHERS WOULD SAY WERE BEST FORGOTTEN.

AT LEAST SOMEDAY I WILL BE ABLE TO SAY
THAT I WAS PROUD OF WHAT I WAS
...A SOLDIER.

GEORGE L. SKYPECK
VIETNAM VETERAN

DEDICATION

This book is dedicated to the families, friends and classmates who shared their memories, stories, and pictures. To all the Pennsylvania Military College graduates we lost in all the wars, thank you for your service to this great country.

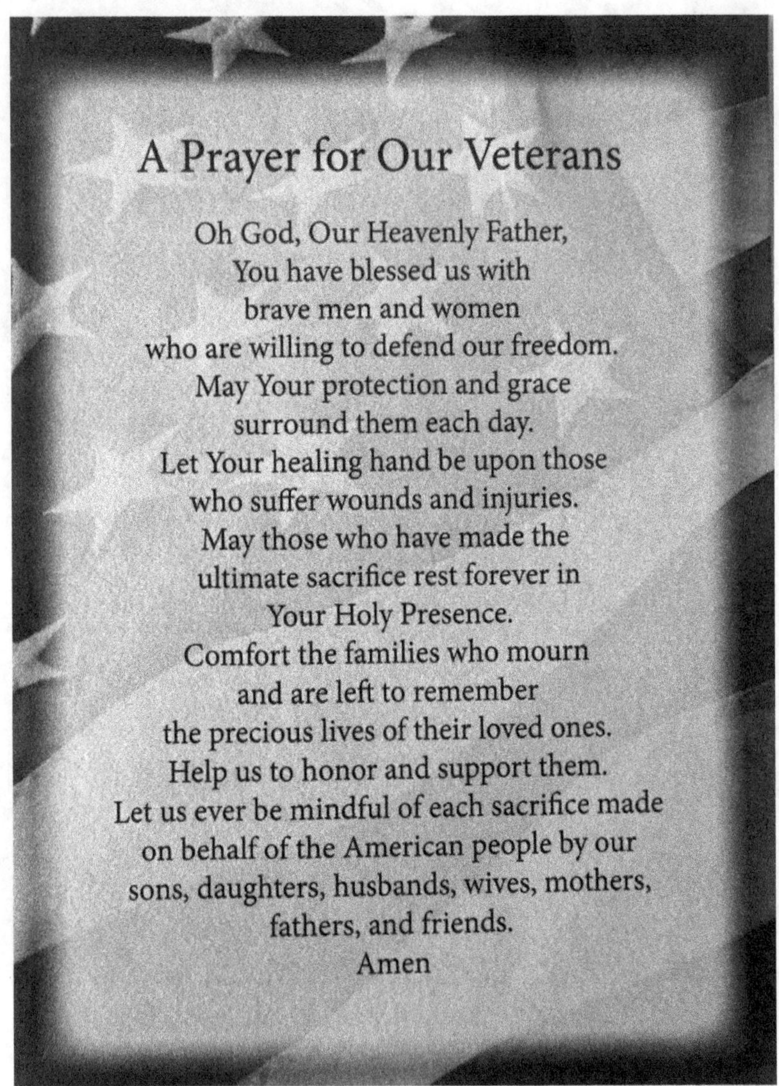

A Prayer for Our Veterans

Oh God, Our Heavenly Father,
You have blessed us with
brave men and women
who are willing to defend our freedom.
May Your protection and grace
surround them each day.
Let Your healing hand be upon those
who suffer wounds and injuries.
May those who have made the
ultimate sacrifice rest forever in
Your Holy Presence.
Comfort the families who mourn
and are left to remember
the precious lives of their loved ones.
Help us to honor and support them.
Let us ever be mindful of each sacrifice made
on behalf of the American people by our
sons, daughters, husbands, wives, mothers,
fathers, and friends.
Amen

PREFACE

While doing research on my first book, *Welcome Home...The Lucky Ones,* I realized there was very little recognition of the ultimate sacrifices made by my fellow Cadet graduates from Pennsylvania Military College who were killed in Vietnam. As a fellow Vietnam Veteran, I understand the unfortunate lack of attention by the American public to this war, and I feel these eight men deserve to be honored for their service. As the title indicates, many of my fellow Vietnam Veterans served bravely and honorably, and 58,281(approximate number in 2023) were killed. Of the eight men I have written about, one had a movie made about his service, *We Were Soldiers,* and another one's service tells a story of heroism, bravery, and leadership that would make a spectacular film. I wanted to put together this book for the families of these eight men, their classmates, the Corps, and all those who served with them in Vietnam.

ACKNOWLEDGMENTS

A special thank you to the widows and families of these eight brave men. Their support via pictures, documents, and sharing stories with me of both the happy and the sad times was invaluable. It must have been difficult for each of you to recall some of these memories. Thank you for your support!

I especially want to thank my wife, Jean, for all her love, support, and encouragement in making this book a reality...*liebe dich!*

Special thanks and appreciation to my Research Librarian, the Assistant Archivist at Widener University's Wolfgram Library, Kayla Van Osten! Kayla's continuous hard work in researching these eight PMC Alumni uncovered articles, photographs, and contact information, and provided me with invaluable leads. Her research was not an easy task. The information was at least sixty years old and showed its age. Kayla, I've said it many times before to you privately, but now I can tell everyone – your work and communications were outstanding. Thank you!

CHAPTER 1: PENNSYLVANIA MILITARY COLLEGE

Before these brave eight men served and gave their lives for this country, they were introduced to military duty life while attending Pennsylvania Military College, PMC. They learned almost everything needed to prepare them for their time in service as leaders and team members who depended on each other when times were difficult.

For all of us graduates of PMC (I was in the Class of '68), no one can ever forget our Rook (freshman) year...Ugh! As a Rook, we were the lowest of the low; we weren't even actually considered a "man" when we entered PMC around the age of 18. Early life as a Rook was chaotic for a while until the upperclassmen arrived and our lives changed. We had a Cadre made up of a sergeant, usually a junior, and a first lieutenant, a first classman (senior), who was the Executive Officer of the Company. They were our teachers and caretakers...and I say that lightly. Who could forget the 2:00 am mattress checks, hitting the walls, duck walks around the dorm hall, squaring around the hall, preparing for Saturday morning inspections, waxing the floors, white glove inspections including unscrewing the light bulbs and looking for dust, bouncing a quarter off your bunk to see if it was made properly and how high it would go, hospital corners, uniforms properly displayed and underwear displayed via 1"x 5" cardboard slats in the clothes locker. Running everywhere, "drop and give me 10" (push-ups), sitting at a brace, and eating square meals, "How's the cow?" (Pass the milk). We can all remember running through the streets of Chester, PA, singing our Army running songs...mostly the clean ones...LOL.

If you are currently having flashbacks, don't worry; so did I, as I tried to remember those glory days. Depending on the time you attended PMC, your memories may differ slightly but close to these. When I look back on our Rook year, despite all its demands on our time, it made us better Cadets because if you could make it through your Rook year, you could make it through almost anything. I didn't mention our drilling or marching on a daily basis, our ROTC Army military staff guiding us via our Military Science Classes under the constant eyes of the school military staff. In our Rook Class, that was Major General Biddle and others. How about the squad or platoon in attack training in Chester Park or Washington Park? I know there are things I am missing, but you get the idea. PMC was military training 24/7 through the school year, especially for the Rooks.

But if you made it through until May of your Rook year, you were recognized as "Old Men" by the upperclassmen...you made it! Your Rook year was demanding from three perspectives. One, it was physically demanding. Two, it was academically challenging trying to adjust to college and PMC military life. Three, it taught you how to manage your time as effectively as possible, this becoming a better person.

The rest of your time at PMC involved many challenges, especially in the '60s due to the Vietnam War, a public that did not support the military or the War, and the constant threat of being drafted. A Cadet at PMC was trained by exceptional military staff members who tried to guide him in the right direction. However, despite their efforts and preparedness, it was a difficult time for all: our uniforms, the pride of following in the footsteps of former Cadets from years past, the Esprit de Corps, the comradery in the Corps, being in a "unique" fraternity whose members were in exclusive company, etc., were all factors in our uncertain future. In our four years at PMC, some of the Cadets had already decided to make the military a career, and the training they received at PMC prepared them well to be effective leaders of the men under their command. Others, like me, started out as Rooks with the mindset of making the military a career; but, that changed when the Vietnam War became a reality and hit home personally. In addition, at the end of our sophomore year, we could see PMC changing direction with the addition of Penn Morton College, a civilian school, to which we lost quite a few Cadets after they switched colleges for whatever reason(s).

In the '60s, PMC was definitely in the beginning stages of transitioning from a military college to a civilian one. However, it did not affect the outstanding preparation we received for our roles as officers in the military, mainly in the US Army but also in the Marine Corps and a few in the Navy. As a PMC Cadet, four years trained you to be an effective leader, fair yet stern, making on-the-spot decisions for the betterment and safety of your men, clearly leading by example, and not asking your men to do something you wouldn't do yourself. It didn't matter which branch of the service you entered. As a PMC graduate, you were trained to be a leader. This training was quite evident during the summer of basic training at Indian Town Gap, PA. Some of our PMC Cadets were cited for exceptional leadership qualities versus the other schools represented.

In the '60s, US troop deployment to South Vietnam increased, and the war began to divide the American public, which affected those going into the service and those already on active duty. When we were commissioned, we signed the blank check we all heard about. Unfortunately, some of those checks should have been marked "paid in full!"

ALL GAVE SOME,
SOME GAVE ALL!

For the eight graduates who paid the ultimate price, for other PMC Cadets, it was time to graduate and be commissioned. With the Vietnam War looming, the future was uncertain one. It would take them down roads not often traveled, but they were expertly and effectively trained and ready to meet the unknown.

Pennsylvania Military College's legacy lives on through the men we honor in this book and all those who lost their lives in all of our country's wars/conflicts.

They served their Country with honor, distinction, bravery, heroism, and the leadership of the men under their command. This book is long overdue, and I hope it does their service to this great country the honor and recognition they deserve.

A quotation by General Charles Hyatt outlines what Pennsylvania Military College was all about:

> When wealth is lost, nothing is lost.
> When health is lost, something is lost.
> When honor is lost, all is lost.

In my opinion, Pennsylvania Military College's Alma Mater says it all:

> Beneath the dome of PMC
> The men in gray march by
> The banners of our loyalty
> Held ever bright and high
> When weary years have called us forth

On home or foreign sod;
The truth you taught shall hold us fast
To country and to God.
Alma Mater, Alma Mater,
ever shall here be,
One corner of our hearts we keep,
In loyal pledge to thee.

In my opinion, the eight graduates who died in Vietnam did not receive the recognition they deserved for serving their country and making the ultimate sacrifice. Many of my fellow PMC Cadets, including myself, served in Vietnam. We weren't welcomed home when we returned...sad but true. These eight men weren't some of the lucky ones who returned to their family and friends to enjoy a happy, healthy, loving life. We lost them at a young age in a country where very few soldiers wanted to be and for a cause that was never made very clear to any of us. But they served with honor, performed their duty bravely without question, and protected themselves and the men they commanded from harm as best they could...even to the cost of losing their own life trying to get their men to safety.

As alumni of Pennsylvania Military College, we are proud of the eight former Cadets for their valor, heroism, and bravery at a time in our country's history when being in Vietnam and serving in the military was not a popular thing for a young man to do. But if we look at PMC's legacy, PMC Cadets have always answered the call to serve this great country and their service must not be forgotten.

In completing the research on these eight men, every attempt was made to contact surviving immediate family members, friends and/or classmates for their feedback and thoughts. All eight men's service experiences were important. However, the amount of archival materials varied for each individual, as did the communications from the contacts we could reach through discussions, pics, and/or documents we obtained.

Pennsylvania Military College was recently honored with a PMC Unit Tribute plaque installed on November 9, 2022, at the National Museum of the United States Army, Fort Belvoir, VA. It was given by the Pennsylvania Military College Class of 1972, the last official class to graduate from PMC. The following demonstrates what PMC meant to us:

> The PMC Corps of Cadets no longer stands in formation or marches on parade, but that gray line still lives on in spirit on those of us who proudly wore Cadet gray.

PENNSYLVANIA
MILITARY COLLEGE
CHESTER, PA
NATION'S SECOND-OLDEST MILITARY COLLEGE
FOUNDED 1821; COLORS CASED 1972
TO FOREVER HONOR AND REMEMBER
THE LEGACY OF
EVERY GRADUATE OF THE CORPS
DEDICATED FOR ALL PMC CADETS
BY THE CLASS OF 1972
VIRTUE, LIBERTY, AND INDEPENDENCE

A LASTING GIFT FROM THE PMC CLASS OF 1972

IT IS WITH GREAT PRIDE THAT ON THE OCCASION OF CELEBRATING OUR 50TH CLASS REUNION THE PENNSYLVANIA MILITARY COLLEGE (PMC) CLASS OF 1972 COMMISSIONED THIS UNIT TRIBUTE AND DEDICATES IT FOR ALL PMC GRADUATES. THIS TRIBUTE WILL BE INSTALLED (TARGET DATE NOV 2022) ALONG THE "PATH OF REMEMBRANCE" BORDERING THE WARRIOR PLAZA AT THE NATIONAL MUSEUM OF THE UNITED STATES ARMY, FORT BELVOIR, VA.

THE VENUE FOR THIS UNIT TRIBUTE WAS SELECTED AS IT PROVIDES A UNIQUE OPPORTUNITY TO PERPETUATE PMC'S LEGACY AND ITS PLACE AND TIME IN HISTORY AS WELL AS THE SERVICE, CONTRIBUTIONS AND ACHIEVEMENTS OF ITS GRADUATES. THIS UNIT TRIBUTE WILL BE VIEWED BY THE MANY VISITORS TO THE MUSEUM FROM ALL OVER THE USA AND THE WORLD. SPECIAL VISITORS WILL BE OUR VETERANS WHO TRAVEL ON HONOR FLIGHTS TO VISIT THE MANY OTHER ICONIC SITES IN THE WASHINGTON DC AREA, SUCH AS ARLINGTON NATIONAL CEMETERY AND WAR MEMORIALS.

THE PMC CORPS OF CADETS NO LONGER STANDS IN FORMATION OR MARCHES ON PARADE, BUT THAT GRAY LINE STILL LIVES ON IN SPIRIT IN THOSE OF US WHO PROUDLY WORE CADET GRAY. AFTER OUR MISSION IN LIFE IS COMPLETED WHEN EACH OF US EXHALES OUR LAST BREATH, THE LEGACY OF PMC WILL BE FOREVER REVERED AND REMEMBERED FOR POSTERITY ALONG WARRIORS PLAZA - A PLACE WHERE THE GENERATIONS WHO COME AFTER US WILL KNOW THAT THE FLAG ONCE FLEW HIGH AND PROUD OVER THE DOME OF PMC.

THANK YOU TO THOSE MEMBERS OF THE PMC CLASS OF 1972 WHO SO GENEROUSLY CONTRIBUTED TO THIS AS A GIFT DEDICATED TO ALL PMC CADETS. WELL DONE!

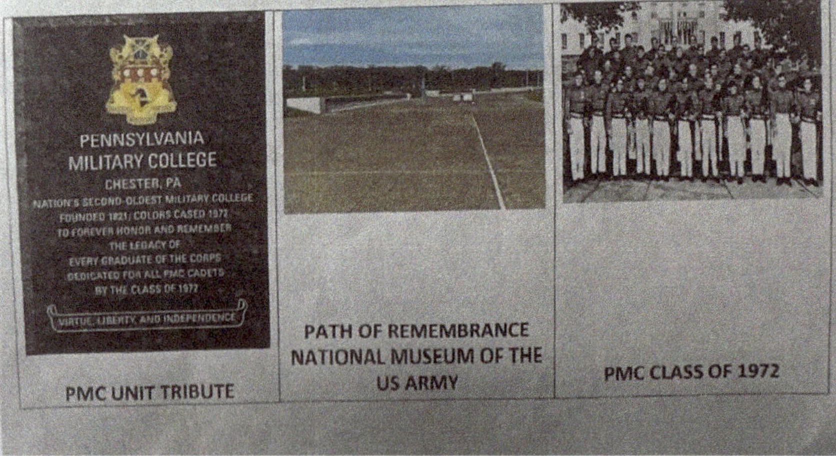
PENNSYLVANIA
MILITARY COLLEGE
CHESTER, PA
NATION'S SECOND-OLDEST MILITARY COLLEGE
FOUNDED 1821; COLORS CASED 1972
TO FOREVER HONOR AND REMEMBER
THE LEGACY OF
EVERY GRADUATE OF THE CORPS
DEDICATED FOR ALL PMC CADETS
BY THE CLASS OF 1972
VIRTUE, LIBERTY, AND INDEPENDENCE

PMC UNIT TRIBUTE

PATH OF REMEMBRANCE NATIONAL MUSEUM OF THE US ARMY

PMC CLASS OF 1972

PMC Color Gvard- Duty, Honor, Country!

It is my hope in the reading of these eight individual stories of valor, heroism, and bravery, we will honor these brave men for their service and the sacrifice they made to our country.

CHAPTER 2: WILLIAM JOHN AHLUM

Bill's Senior Yearbook picture.

William "Bill" Ahlum, son of Mr. and Mrs. Claude L. Ahlum, was raised in Hatboro, PA. Bill had a brother, Leon, 15 months older, who the family called Lee. According to Lee, "Bill liked to play baseball, was a good student but bright when it came to engineering." They both attended Upper Moreland High School. Bill graduated in 1961. Bill had applied to Pennsylvania Military College, now Widener, in Chester, PA, and joined as a Rook in the Class of '66.

HONORED . . . Cadet William Ahlum, at left, 5-3 High Ave., Hatboro, was designated a distinguished military student at ceremonies held April 17 at Pennsylvania Military College. Congratulating him are Col. Samuel Smith, center, professor of military science at PMC, and Lt. Gen. John L. Throckmorton, chief, office of reserve components, U.S. Army. Cadet Ahlum is a senior at the college.

Bill was an engineering student, a member of SAE (the Society of Automotive Engineers), and enjoyed intramural sports. I had the good fortune of pledging Tau Kappa Epsilon (TKE) my sophomore year and I had the privilege of having Bill as my Big Brother. One of his greatest joys, if not the greatest, was to be a TKE brother. As my Big Brother, he was always there for me and took the time to listen to my issues. Pledging a fraternity as a Cadet was a little more trying than at a normal college. Bill was always there, giving me advice, supporting me, recommending how to manage my time more efficiently and effectively, and counseling me on how to deal with some of the other Brothers. In the end, I made it as his Brother. I couldn't have done it without him. Bill was a great guy, well respected, and loved by his TKE Brothers...YITB...Ken.

In the summer of 1963, Bill and the former Donna Penn of Oreland, PA, met at a summer job at Link Belt Co. in Philadelphia, PA. Bill's dad worked there as well as a neighbor of Donna's. If Donna remembered correctly, Bill was entering his junior year at PMC and she was a freshman at Muhlenberg College in Allentown, PA. Bill asked Donna out several times before she accepted. They finally went downtown Philadelphia to a movie. Bill was active in his fraternity, TKE, and they attended some parties. Donna withdrew from college her sophomore year and then worked full time at Link Belt. They continued to date.

The couple broke up for a while. Bill's dad recommended that Bill, who still had feelings for Donna, should pick her up after work...he did. He waited for her at the train station in his VW Beetle. When she got into the car, Bill asked Donna to get him a piece of gum out of the glove compartment. Attached to the piece of gum was his fraternity pin, and, as Donna recalled, "memories."

Donna's parents, Mr. and Mrs. John Penn of Oreland, PA., announced the engagement. Bill graduated and was commissioned on June 4, 1966, as a second lieutenant (RA -Regular Army) in the Ordnance Branch.

On September 10, 1966, they were married at Christ Lutheran Church in Oreland, PA. John Finn was the Best Man and Bill's brother, Claude (Leon) Ahlum, Jr., was an attendant. The music was provided by a band called The Runabouts from PMC made up of all TKE brothers. When the wedding was over, the newlyweds went on their honeymoon to Acapulco and Mexico City. When they returned, they temporarily moved in with Bill's parents while he waited for his assignment orders.

In the fall of 1966, Bill was assigned to the Engineer Officers Basic Class at Fort Belvoir, VA. Upon completion of the course, Bill had selected Germany for his next assignment. In March of 1967, Bill was assigned to a unit based in Kaiserslautern, Germany. Donna went with him. While Bill worked with the military, Donna was lucky enough and got on the economy (working with Germans) for Harry's Gift Shop who sold high end gifts to American officer's wives. Donna said she enjoyed her work and it kept her busy.

Bill's PMC Days

Junior Ring Dance At PMC- Bill & Donna

While on their honeymoon in Acapulco

This was of Bill while stationed in Germany

Bill was transferred to Mannheim, Germany, to the 53rd Ordnance Group.

While in Germany, Bill received his first Army Commendation Medal for meritorious service in a tracked vehicle Maintenance Battalion. His final assignment was as an intelligence and operations officer and adjutant for Headquarters, U.S. Army Europe. Bill was very proud of his collection of German beer glasses that Donna had in a display case until three years ago. While in Germany, Bill purchased his dream car, a white Porsche. Unfortunately, it was totaled by a drunk German who ran a red light and broadsided it. As Donna said, "We went back to a VW Beetle." Bill was in Germany for 19 months before he was transferred back to the US.

Bill returned to the US in October 1968, the same month he was promoted to Captain, and was assigned to Aberdeen Proving Grounds in Maryland for three months. From there, he was assigned to Vietnam.

Donna said, "Before he left, he told me we would start a family when he returned, so he could be there with me to raise our children. He had also told his parents that he planned to make the Army his career. I remained with my parents in Oreland...waiting for his return."

In a letter written to his parents, Bill wrote:

> If every person in civilian life had one-half the loyalty to their job and their country [compared to the type of person serving in the U. S. Armed Forces], we would truly be the greatest country now and for all time to come.

Bill receives his second Army Commendation Medal in Vietnam just before his death

Bill arrived in Vietnam on February 9, 1969, and was assigned to the 630th Ordnance Company, 184th Ordnance Battalion, Army Support Command, Qui Nhon, Vietnam. On March 23, 1969, in Binh Dinh province, at approximately 23:15 (11:15 pm), Bill's unit came under attack by an enemy force of unknown size with small arms, mortars, rockets, and automatic weapons fire. Captain Ahlum repeatedly risked his own life evacuating his men and assisting the wounded from the area. The attack ignited a fire that caused an ammunition dump explosion. Captain Ahlum, SP4 Jerry Peterson, and SPS Michael Berry were killed. Captain Bill Ahlum was only 25 years old and had only been in country six weeks.

On April 23, 1969, funeral services were held for Captain Ahlum at Christ Lutheran Church, in Oreland, PA. Bill was buried at the Beverly National Cemetery, Grave 461, Section V, in Beverly, New Jersey. Acting as pallbearers were PMC Cadets and TKE Brothers Ron Sayers, Ted Prociv, Dave Mancini, James Simonelli, David Ling, and Frank Giorno. Bill was survived by his wife, the former Donna N. Penn, his parents, Mr. and Mrs. Claude Ahlum, and his brother Leon.

Memorial Service for Bill in Vietnam

DEPARTMENT OF THE ARMY
OFFICE OF THE ADJUTANT GENERAL
WASHINGTON, D. C. 20315

AGPB-AC Ahlum, William J.
SSAN 188-34-3264 (23 Mar 69)

23 JUN 1970

Mrs. Donna M. Ahlum
332 Lyster Road
Oreland, Pennsylvania 19075

Dear Mrs. Ahlum:

I have the honor to inform you that the Government of the Republic of Vietnam has awarded posthumously to your husband the National Order of Vietnam, Fifth Class and the Gallantry Cross with Palm.

Arrangements are being made to have these awards delivered to you in the near future by a representative of the Commanding General, First United States Army.

The representative selected will communicate with you in the next few weeks to arrange for delivery. Any inquiry or correspondence concerning delivery should be addressed to the Commanding General, First United States Army, Fort George G. Meade, Maryland 20755.

My continued sympathy is with you.

Sincerely,

Kenneth G. Wickham

KENNETH G. WICKHAM
Major General, USA
The Adjutant General

1984

NOVEMBER

Norristown Vietnam War Memorial

This Monument was erected by the residents and the businesses of the Borough of Norristown to pay tribute and Honor to all those who sacrificed their lives and to all those who served our Country in the Vietnam War.

We dedicate this Memorial to the Memory of those who lost their lives from Norristown and throughout the entire region of Montgomery County.

Charles Dewees
Chairman and Founder

* Bill Ahlum was honored for his sacrifice.

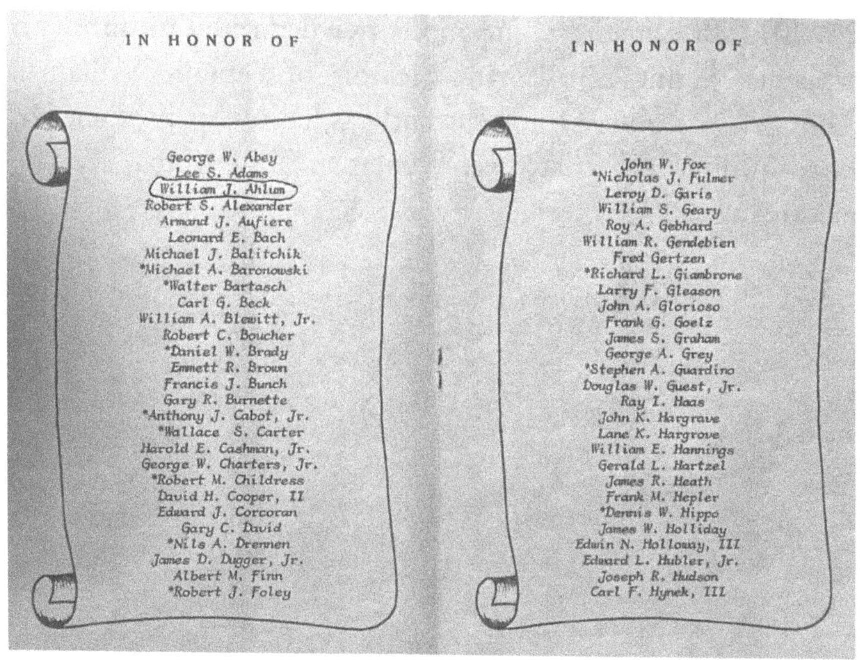

IN HONOR OF

George W. Abey
Lee S. Adams
William J. Ahlum
Robert S. Alexander
Armand J. Aufiere
Leonard E. Bach
Michael J. Balitchik
*Michael A. Baronowski
*Walter Bartasch
Carl G. Beck
William A. Blewitt, Jr.
Robert C. Boucher
*Daniel W. Brady
Emmett R. Brown
Francis J. Bunch
Gary R. Burnette
*Anthony J. Cabot, Jr.
*Wallace S. Carter
Harold E. Cashman, Jr.
George W. Charters, Jr.
*Robert M. Childress
David H. Cooper, II
Edward J. Corcoran
Gary C. David
*Nils A. Drennen
James D. Dugger, Jr.
Albert M. Finn
*Robert J. Foley

IN HONOR OF

John W. Fox
*Nicholas J. Fulmer
Leroy D. Garis
William S. Geary
Roy A. Gebhard
William R. Gendebien
Fred Gertzen
*Richard L. Giambrone
Larry F. Gleason
John A. Glorioso
Frank G. Goelz
James S. Graham
George A. Grey
*Stephen A. Guardino
Douglas W. Guest, Jr.
Ray I. Haas
John K. Hargrave
Lane K. Hargrove
William E. Hannings
Gerald L. Hartzel
James R. Heath
Frank M. Hepler
*Dennis W. Hippo
James W. Holliday
Edwin N. Holloway, III
Edward L. Hubler, Jr.
Joseph R. Hudson
Carl F. Hynek, III

On August 21, 1969, The Bronze Star for Valor and the Purple Heart were awarded posthumously to Captain Ahlum at ceremonies held at PMC. The medals were accepted by his widow Donna from Colonel Ford Fuller, the commandant of the Cadet Corps of Pennsylvania Military College. Also present were Bill's parents, Mr. and Mrs. Claude Ahlum.

I was serving in the US Army in Germany from 1969 - 1971 and never knew Bill was killed until I returned from Germany in August of 1971 prior to going to Vietnam in September 1971. I had lost two close friends in Vietnam and their losses affected my future plans about staying in the service as a career. They were only 23 and 25 years old – gone so young and for what? My decision was made.

Bill was honored at his 50th High School Reunion at Upper Moreland High School Class of 1961, on Tuesday, October

25, 2011, by a memorial magnolia tree dedicated to him with a plaque reading: "In Loving Memory of Captain William J. Ahlum, Class of 1961." The event was led by his brother, Dr. Leon Ahlum and State Representative Tom Murt. See the picture below.

From left to right: Captain William Ahlum's widow, Donna Groat, her husband, Gary, behind her, Bill's brother, Dr. Leon Ahlum to the right.

In an article written about this event by Theresa Katalinas, "Local Soldier Killed in Vietnam," she refers to a speech given by then State Rep. Thomas P. Murt. In it he said," Ahlum was very proud of being a soldier."

In 2016, at Bill's 50th Class of 1966 Reunion event at PMC, Thom Chiomento, representing the Class, presented the Reunion Medallions to the PMC Museum that depicted three white crosses on one side to honor the three Classmates lost in Vietnam: Ahlum, Wilson, and Isom. See the pics that follow.

On July 1, 2020, the General Assembly of Pennsylvania designated a portion of County line Road (SR 2038) between N. Warminster Road and Newton Road in Hatboro, PA (Bucks County), as the Captain William J. Ahlum Memorial Highway.

Bill was 25 years old at the time of his death. Donna helped me immensely in pulling together the pieces of the puzzle so the readers can get a better understanding of Bill. I will close this chapter with a comment from Donna:

> In writing this, I had a wonderful trip down the proverbial memory lane. And now that I'm at the end of my story, I'm in tears. Bill was my first love. There were so many aspects of him ...the playboy, the family man, and my military hero. He will be in my heart forever.

CLASS OF 66 - 50th REUNION
HOMECOMING 2016
"The Best Class"
Pennsylvania Military College

Beneath the Dome of PMC
Ahlum
Wilson
Isom
DUTY•HONOR•GOD•COUNTRY

3/2/23, 7:09 PM Act of Jul. 1, 2020,P.L. 548, No. 47 Cl. 87 - MULTIPLE DESIGNATIONS IN MULTIPLE COUNTIES - DESIGNATION

the state each day to rescue Pennsylvanians in distress."

(b) Designation.--The bridge on I-70 in Westmoreland County over the Youghiogheny River is designated the Matthew Smelser Memorial Bridge in both directions.

(c) Signs.--The Department of Transportation shall erect and maintain appropriate signs displaying the name of the highway to traffic in both directions on the highway.

Section 10. Captain William J. Ahlum Memorial Highway.

(a) Findings.--The General Assembly finds and declares as follows:

(1) On March 23, 1969, Captain William John Ahlum of Hatboro was killed in Vietnam.

(2) Captain Ahlum served in the United States Army and was a commissioned officer through The Pennsylvania Military College, now Widener University, in Chester.

(3) Captain Ahlum was in Vietnam for only a few weeks when he was killed in Binh Dinh Province, South Vietnam.

(4) At the time of his death, Captain Ahlum was serving in the 1st Logistical Command, 184th Ordnance Battalion.

(5) Captain Ahlum was the recipient of the Purple Heart, National Defense Medal, Vietnam Campaign Medal, Vietnam Service Medal, Distinguished Service Medal, Vietnam Gallantry Cross Unit Citation and Good Conduct Medal.

(b) Designation.--The portion of County Line Road (SR 2038) between N. Warminster Road and Newtown Road in Bucks County is designated the Captain William J. Ahlum Memorial Highway.

(c) Signs.--The Department of Transportation shall erect and maintain appropriate signs displaying the name of the highway to traffic in both directions on the highway.

Section 11. Specialist 4 Harold E. Cashman Memorial Highway.

(a) Findings.--The General Assembly finds and declares as follows:

(1) Harold E. Cashman was attending Delaware Valley College in Doylestown full-time when he received his draft notice in 1967.

(2) Instead of requesting a student deferment to which he was entitled, he reported for his conscription into the United States Army.

(3) After completion of his Basic Training, Specialist 4 Harold E. Cashman was assigned to the elite 1st Cavalry Division and deployed to South Vietnam in August 1967.

(4) On January 31, 1968, he was killed in Quang Tri Province, South Vietnam, on the first day of the infamous Tet Offensive.

(b) Designation.--The portion of County Line Road (SR 2038) between N. Warminster Road and Jacksonville Road in Bucks County is designated the Specialist 4 Harold E. Cashman Memorial Highway.

(c) Signs.--The Department of Transportation shall erect and maintain appropriate signs displaying the name of the highway to traffic in both directions on the highway.

Section 12. Effective date.

This act shall take effect in 60 days.

3/2/23, 7:08 PM Act of Jul. 1, 2020,P.L. 548, No. 47 Cl. 87 - MULTIPLE DESIGNATIONS IN MULTIPLE COUNTIES - DESIGNATION

MULTIPLE DESIGNATIONS IN MULTIPLE COUNTIES - DESIGNATION

Act of Jul. 1, 2020, P.L. 548, No. 47 Cl. 87

An Act

Designating the highway interchange of U.S. Route 222 with Mohns Hill Road, Cumru Township, Berks County, as the Corporal Mahlon L. Fink Iwo Jima Memorial Highway Interchange; designating the portion of State Route 1015, also known as Knights Road, between State Route 63 and U.S. Route 13 in the City of Philadelphia as the Sergeant James O'Connor IV Memorial Highway; designating a bridge, identified as Bridge Key 57213, carrying State Route 1036 over Six Mile Run, Broad Top Township, Bedford County, as the Sergeant David Leon Barber Memorial Bridge; designating a bridge, identified as Bridge Key 52785, on that portion of State Route 4027 over Bald Eagle Creek, Snyder Township, Blair County, as the Cpl. Donald L. Westley Memorial Bridge; designating the bridge, identified as Bridge Key 48976, on that portion of Pennsylvania Route 669 that crosses the Casselman River at the west end of Ord Street, Salisbury Borough, Somerset County, as the Sergeant Stephen M. Minick Memorial Bridge; designating the bridge, identified as Bridge Key 31586, on that portion of State Route 2004 carrying Broadway Street over the Casselman River in Summit Township, Somerset County, as the Airman Michael L. Menser Memorial Bridge; designating a bridge, identified as Bridge Key 15279, on that portion of State Route 2025, also known as Morton Avenue, over Stony Creek in Morton Borough, Delaware County, as the Captain Michael Malinowski, Sr., Memorial Bridge; designating a portion of State Route 2012 in Monroe County as the Reverend Dr. Bishop William Earl Lee Highway; designating the bridge on I-70 in Westmoreland County over the Youghiogheny River as the Matthew Smelser Memorial Bridge; designating the portion of County Line Road (SR 2038) between N. Warminster Road and Newtown Road in Bucks County as the Captain William J. Ahlum Memorial Highway; and designating the portion of County Line Road (SR 2038) between N. Warminster Road and Jacksonville Road in Bucks County as the Specialist 4 Harold E. Cashman Memorial Highway.

The General Assembly of the Commonwealth of Pennsylvania hereby enacts as follows:

Section 1. Corporal Mahlon L. Fink Iwo Jima Memorial Highway Interchange.

(a) Findings.--The General Assembly finds and declares as follows:

(1) Mahlon L. Fink lived a life of dedicated and humble service to his community and to this Commonwealth.

(2) Mr. Fink was born December 1, 1925, in what is now the Daniel Boone Homestead.

(3) Mr. Fink was a student at Reading High School, when he was compelled by a sense of duty to join the war effort. He dropped out of school following his sophomore year and joined the United States Marine Corps on his 18th birthday.

(4) Mr. Fink was a member of the 5th Marine Division in the Pacific Theater.

(5) Mr. Fink and his company landed on Iwo Jima on February 16, 1945, as one of the first units in combat.

(6) On the 12th day of combat, Mr. Fink was injured when a mortar round fell near him sending shrapnel into his legs. As a result of his injuries. Mr. Fink was awarded the Purple Heart.

22

William John Ahlum

Captain

630TH ORD CO, 184TH ORD BN, ARMY SPT CMD QUI NHON, 1ST LOG CMD, USARV

Army of the United States

Hatboro, Pennsylvania

January 22, 1944 to March 23, 1969

WILLIAM J AHLUM is on the Wall at Panel W28, Line 16

See the full profile or name rubbing for William Ahlum

23 Nov 2007

REMEMBERED

by another 184th Ordnance Battalion veteran 1968-1969.
dennisheim@insightbb.com

A Note from The Virtual Wall

The MACV Summary for March 1969 contains the following entry for 23 March:

> - IPFV (BINH DINH PROV) - At approx 2315, 2 US Army cbt svc spt units based in the same area about 5 mi SW of Qui Nhong were atkd by unk size en forces. The en empl SA & auto wpns fire while the trps rtn fire with organic wpns. Contact was lost at an unreptd time when the en withdrew. No en were reptd to have pent the peri. En losses are unknown. A fire which was started during the act caused lt mat dam at 1 loc. US cas were 3 kd & 32 wounded.

The three men killed were from the 184th Ordnance Battalion:

- **630th Ordnance Co:**
  - **CPT William J. Ahlum, Hatboro, PA**
  - **SP4 Jerry L. Peterson, La Porte, IN (Bronze Star "V")**
- **820th Ordnance Co:**
  - **SP5 Michael L. Berry, Ashley, IN**

THE VIRTUAL WALL ® VIETNAM VETERANS MEMORIAL www.VIRTUALWALL.org

Contact Us © Copyright 1997-2019 www.VirtualWall.org, Ltd ®(TM) Last update 09/12/2019.

2/16/23, 9:05 AM www.VirtualWall.org Profile

William John Ahlum

ON THE WALL: **Panel W28 Line 16**

This page Copyright© 1997-2018 www.VirtualWall.org Ltd.

PERSONAL DATA:

Home of Record:	Hatboro, PA
Date of birth:	01/22/1944

MILITARY DATA:

Service Branch:	Army of the United States
Grade at loss:	O3
Rank:	Captain
Promotion Note:	None
ID No:	OF109675
MOS:	4514: Conventional Ammunition Office
Length Service:	04
Unit:	630TH ORD CO, 184TH ORD BN, ARMY SPT CMD QUI NHON, 1ST LOG CMD, USARV

CASUALTY DATA:

Start Tour:	02/09/1969
Incident Date:	03/23/1969
Casualty Date:	03/23/1969
Status Date:	Not Applicable
Status Change:	Not Applicable
Age at Loss:	25
Location:	Binh Dinh Province, South Vietnam
Remains:	Body recovered
Repatriated:	Not Applicable
Identified:	Not Applicable
Casualty Type:	Hostile, died outright
Casualty Reason:	Ground casualty
Casualty Detail:	Burns

URL: https://VirtualWall.org/da/AhlumWJ01a.htm

Data accessed: 2/16/2023

THE VIRTUAL WALL ® **www.VirtualWall.org**

Print This Page Close This Page

Page template 10/09/2015

CHAPTER 3:
ROBERT HENRY ALDRICH

Bob grew up in Great Neck, Long Island, NY, where he attended Great Neck South High School and won the John Philip Sousa Music Award at graduation. He had a younger brother named Donnie Aldrich who supposedly now lives in Florida. Attempts to find him were not successful. Most of the research on Bob focuses around his four years at Pennsylvania Military College and his time in the service.

Bob's senior picture from his yearbook...Class of 1969.

Bob was very active while a Cadet at PMC...here are some of the organizations he belonged to:

- Committee member of the Canterbury Club: "The Canterbury Club is an organization for the people of college age in the Episcopal Church. It is designed primarily to bring the students of the area together and give them an outlet for the discussion of common problems, to offer them the opportunity of hearing outside authorities and help them keep up with current religious activities within and outside the church."
- He was First Sergeant in the PMC ROTC Company of the Association of the United States Army (AUSA).
- He was a member of the 15th Regimental Headquarters – Pershing Rifles as the Public Information Officer.
- He was a member of the Ranger Platoon as the Assistant Training Officer.
- Unit Leader of Bersaglieri: The BERSAGLIERI is a functional organization within the Corps of Cadets whose primary aim is to develop and promote unity, esprit, and honor among the Cadets through the medium of proficiency in all aspects of the US Army Special Forces such as guerilla warfare, karate, physical conditioning and coordination, and devotion to duty. A physical examination and parental consent are two of the prerequisites for membership.

Dennis (who later changed his name to Erik) Bolton and Bob were very close friends as well as classmates. The following picture shows the two of them getting ready for a room inspection in the dorm, Howell Hall, at PMC during their junior year. They were roommates in Alpha Company. Bob was First Sergeant and Erik was a Sergeant Squad Leader.

Erik Bolton (left) and Bob.

Both young men were focused on joining the United States Marine Corps upon graduation. In the picture below, these PMC Cadets had also shown interest in the Marine Corps and even wore the eagle globe and anchor insignia on their Delta

Cadet Uniforms...being worn in the photo. In the center of the pic is the Marine Corps Colonel, who was from the Officer Selection Office at the Philadelphia Naval Base where they joined up in April 1968. To the Colonel's left is Bob Aldrich, Lieutenant Platoon Commander. To the Colonel's right is Erik Bolton, Provost Marshal Lieutenant.

One of Bob's friends and Classmates was Jim Hogg. Jim talks about Bob, Erik Bolton and Tom Childers always being together. Erik called them the "ABC boys."

Jim remembers an instance with Bob during their first month of training/hazing. There was a competition for the best company called "gymkana." Bob and Jim were competing to see who could do the most curls with a 100-pound barbell. Jim won by one with 25. Dave Duthie wrote a letter to Jim's file that his performance was the key to Charlie Company placing first. Jim said he and Aldrich were never close after that. Bob continued to work out and by graduation he had to have all his uniforms altered. Jim said he started to look like Arnold Schwarzenegger. Jim also said Bob Aldrich was an outstanding officer who gave his life in service to our country.

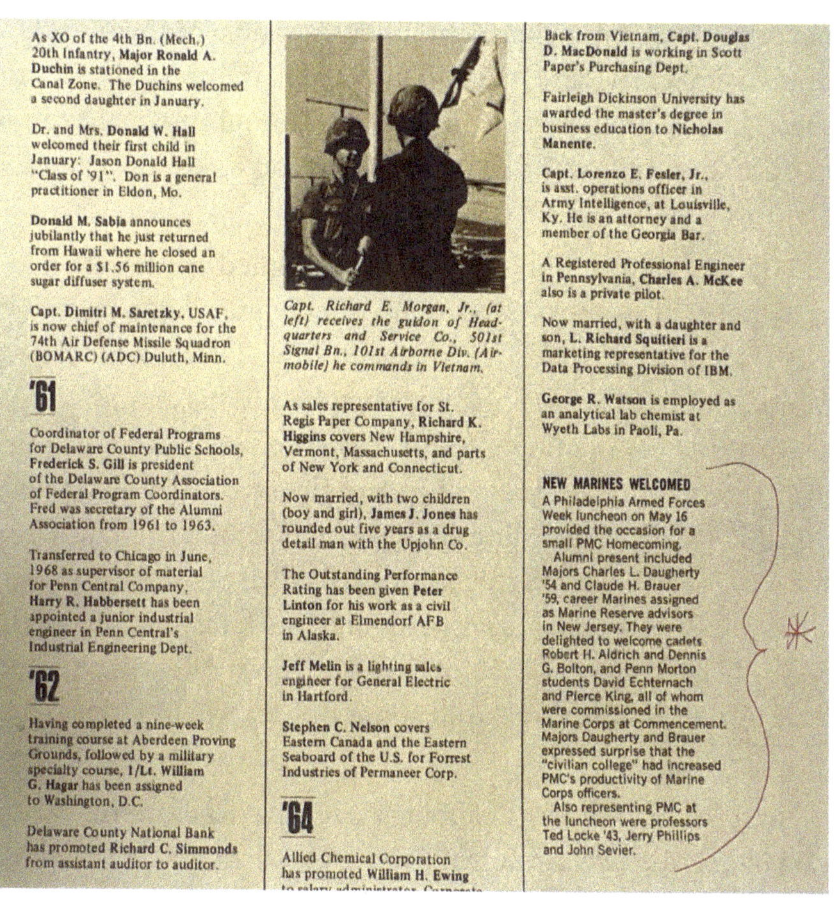

As XO of the 4th Bn. (Mech.) 20th Infantry, **Major Ronald A. Duchin** is stationed in the Canal Zone. The Duchins welcomed a second daughter in January.

Dr. and Mrs. **Donald W. Hall** welcomed their first child in January: Jason Donald Hall "Class of '91". Don is a general practitioner in Eldon, Mo.

Donald M. Sabia announces jubilantly that he just returned from Hawaii where he closed an order for a $1.56 million cane sugar diffuser system.

Capt. Dimitri M. Saretzky, USAF, is now chief of maintenance for the 74th Air Defense Missile Squadron (BOMARC) (ADC) Duluth, Minn.

'61

Coordinator of Federal Programs for Delaware County Public Schools, **Frederick S. Gill** is president of the Delaware County Association of Federal Program Coordinators. Fred was secretary of the Alumni Association from 1961 to 1963.

Transferred to Chicago in June, 1968 as supervisor of material for Penn Central Company, **Harry R. Habbersett** has been appointed a junior industrial engineer in Penn Central's Industrial Engineering Dept.

'62

Having completed a nine-week training course at Aberdeen Proving Grounds, followed by a military specialty course, **1/Lt. William G. Hagar** has been assigned to Washington, D.C.

Delaware County National Bank has promoted **Richard C. Simmonds** from assistant auditor to auditor.

Capt. Richard E. Morgan, Jr., (at left) receives the guidon of Headquarters and Service Co., 501st Signal Bn., 101st Airborne Div. (Airmobile) he commands in Vietnam.

As sales representative for St. Regis Paper Company, **Richard K. Higgins** covers New Hampshire, Vermont, Massachusetts, and parts of New York and Connecticut.

Now married, with two children (boy and girl), **James J. Jones** has rounded out five years as a drug detail man with the Upjohn Co.

The Outstanding Performance Rating has been given **Peter Linton** for his work as a civil engineer at Elmendorf AFB in Alaska.

Jeff Melin is a lighting sales engineer for General Electric in Hartford.

Stephen C. Nelson covers Eastern Canada and the Eastern Seaboard of the U.S. for Forrest Industries of Permaneer Corp.

'64

Allied Chemical Corporation has promoted **William H. Ewing**

Back from Vietnam, **Capt. Douglas D. MacDonald** is working in Scott Paper's Purchasing Dept.

Fairleigh Dickinson University has awarded the master's degree in business education to **Nicholas Manente**.

Capt. Lorenzo E. Fesler, Jr., is asst. operations officer in Army Intelligence, at Louisville, Ky. He is an attorney and a member of the Georgia Bar.

A Registered Professional Engineer in Pennsylvania, **Charles A. McKee** also is a private pilot.

Now married, with a daughter and son, **L. Richard Squitieri** is a marketing representative for the Data Processing Division of IBM.

George R. Watson is employed as an analytical lab chemist at Wyeth Labs in Paoli, Pa.

NEW MARINES WELCOMED

A Philadelphia Armed Forces Week luncheon on May 16 provided the occasion for a small PMC Homecoming.

Alumni present included Majors Charles L. Daugherty '54 and Claude H. Brauer '59, career Marines assigned as Marine Reserve advisors in New Jersey. They were delighted to welcome cadets Robert H. Aldrich and Dennis G. Bolton, and Penn Morton students David Echternach and Pierce King, all of whom were commissioned in the Marine Corps at Commencement. Majors Daugherty and Brauer expressed surprise that the "civilian college" had increased PMC's productivity of Marine Corps officers.

Also representing PMC at the luncheon were professors Ted Locke '43, Jerry Phillips and John Sevier.

Impact Mag, 1969

According to Erik Bolton, he, Bob Aldrich, and Tom Childers, got a ride to the Philadelphia Naval Base Marine Corps Barracks' Officer Selection Office, raised their right hands and committed themselves to the Marine Corps in April 1968. That summer, they went to Quantico, and spent 12 weeks at OCS. They graduated near the top of their class. One day prior to their PMC Commencement, they were commissioned as Second Lieutenants in the Marine Corps in their dress whites amid a sea of Army greens by a Marine Corps Colonel from the Naval Base. He thinks that was May 30, 1969. The next day was Commencement. Then the three of them went to The Basic School at Quantico and spent the next six months there. Bob Aldrich went to helicopter training and qualification in Alabama. Erik went to the Marine Corps Armor School in California.

1st Lieutenant Bob Aldrich was assigned to the 7th Fleet as a pilot of a Marine Medium Helicopter Squadron 165. On December 27, 1971, at the age of 24, 1st Lt. Aldrich was piloting a C-46D (Sea Knight), when he and his crew, were lost at sea while conducting a sector search to watch Russian ships near the fleet in the Indian Ocean. The wreckage suggested a possible mechanical failure causing the helicopter to crash into the sea. Also aboard were co-pilot LT Allen Scurlock and crew chief LCPL Gregory Davis. All suffered fatal injuries in the crash. Davis's body was recovered but those of the two pilots were not. Erik Bolton was told about Bob's death in a letter from his parents.

In a letter Bob wrote about sixteen days before his death, Bob had written to a group of third and fourth graders in which he expressed appreciation for cookies they had sent.

> I take a great deal of pride in being a Marine serving over here so young kids like yourselves will be free to do as you choose and live in a free country: the greatest country

in the world. Being younger than myself and living your whole life in the United States, you do not realize how good you really have it. Most Americans take America for granted. I know I did until I came over here and saw how the rest of the people in the world live. Never be ashamed of the United States. It's the greatest – and I will always be proud of being an American."

This letter appeared in the *PMC Alumni Magazine* in 1972.

On January 17, 1972, the following letter was sent from Gerard T. Frey, LTC, USA (Ret), Commandant, Pennsylvania Military College Corps of Cadets, to Bob's parents, Mr. & Mrs. Henry M. Aldrich.

17 January 1972

Mr. & Mrs. Henry M. Aldrich
Harris & Aldrich Sales, Inc.
320 Northern Boulevard
Great Neck, New York 11021

Dear Mr. & Mrs. Aldrich:

I only knew Robert a few months but I remember him.

My staff all knew him well and your letter was a shock to us all.

I was wounded in VietNam and spent two and one half years in Army hospitals. I spent a lot of time with the badly wounded and through it all I discovered one great truth – those who give all they have to give for their country give it willingly. I have seen soldiers weep when they are in the hospital and always they wept for someone else – the ones who did not make it. Horribly wounded young wrecks of manhood who passed off their own suffering lightly as "no big thing" and yet who held my hand as we cried together for hours for someone else.

The good ones – the ones who value their country over self – give all they have every day. They want to live but are prepared to die. They would not have it any other way.

For whatever comfort it is worth, I'm sure Robert wanted to be where he was doing his duty.

I wish I could lighten your grief but I know words have no meaning. I do know that his sacrifice was for something.

We will fly the flag at half-mast for him this week. When the Corps returns in February we will hold a memorial service for him.

. & Mrs. Henry M. Aldrich -2-

I am so sorry. I pray that God will ease your grief. The rps joins me in offering you our prayers for his soul.

You are not alone - he belonged to us, too.

Sincerely,

GERARD T. FREY
LTC, USA (Ret)
Commandant

On Saturday, February 19, 1972, at 9:00am, a memorial service was held at St. Paul's Episcopal Church, 9th and Madison Streets, Chester, PA. The service reportedly had 275 members of the PMC Cadet Corps, the school concert choir, and band. The service was conducted by the Reverend Harold Guy, Chief Chaplain at PMC Colleges. Please see the program for the service on the next page.

Due Bob Aldrich's death occurring at sea and not in Vietnam, his name was initially not put on The Wall in Washington, DC. However, in a *New York Times* article (March 11, 1986), Bob was listed as one of 108 Americans killed in the Vietnam War scheduled to be added. In another article about the same subject, Bob's mother, Debbie, stated:

> I know he'd be pleased to know his name is going to be included. All they ever told us was that he was lost on

a classified mission in a classified area. We never found him. We think he was lost at sea.

Mrs. Aldrich relates how they found out about Bob's death:

Her husband, Hank, first saw the Marine officer who informed them through the window. We knew exactly what was happening. I went to the door, I opened it, and I just said, 'What's happened to Bob?'" All our Christmas decorations, including the tree, were still up. Of course, Christmas has never been an enjoyable time for us since.

Bob was 24...gone too soon. RIP my Cadet and Vietnam Veteran Brother...you are not forgotten!

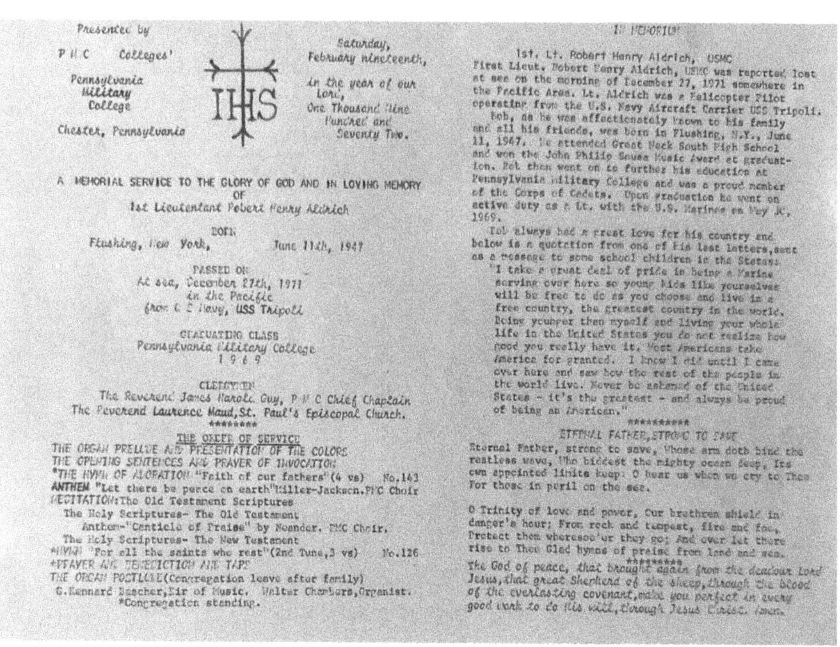

Presented by
P M C Colleges'
Pennsylvania
Military
College
Chester, Pennsylvania

IHS

Saturday,
February nineteenth,
in the year of our
Lord,
One Thousand Nine
Hundred and
Seventy Two.

A MEMORIAL SERVICE TO THE GLORY OF GOD AND IN LOVING MEMORY
OF
1st Lieutenant Robert Henry Aldrich

BORN
Flushing, New York, June 11th, 1947

PASSED ON
At sea, December 27th, 1971
in the Pacific
from U S Navy, USS Tripoli

GRADUATING CLASS
Pennsylvania Military College
1 9 6 9

CLERGYMEN
The Reverend James Harold Guy, P M C Chief Chaplain
The Reverend Laurence Maud, St. Paul's Episcopal Church.
****

THE ORDER OF SERVICE
THE ORGAN PRELUDE AND PRESENTATION OF THE COLORS
THE OPENING SENTENCES AND PRAYER OF INVOCATION
*THE HYMN OF ADORATION "Faith of our fathers" (4 vs) No.143
ANTHEM "Let there be peace on earth" Miller-Jackson. PMC Choir
RECITATION: The Old Testament Scriptures
The Holy Scriptures- The Old Testament
Anthem-"Canticle of Praise" by Neander. PMC Choir.
The Holy Scriptures- The New Testament
*HYMN "For all the saints who rest" (2nd Tune, 3 vs) No.126
*PRAYER AND BENEDICTION AND TAPS
THE ORGAN POSTLUDE (Congregation leave after family)
G. Kennard Bascher, Dir of Music. Walter Chambers, Organist.
*Congregation standing.

IN MEMORIAM

1st. Lt. Robert Henry Aldrich, USMC

First Lieut. Robert Henry Aldrich, USMC was reported lost at sea on the morning of December 27, 1971 somewhere in the Pacific Area. Lt. Aldrich was a Helicopter Pilot operating from the U.S. Navy Aircraft Carrier USS Tripoli.

Bob, as he was affectionately known to his family and all his friends, was born in Flushing, N.Y., June 11, 1947. He attended Great Neck South High School and won the John Philip Sousa Music Award at graduation. Bob then went on to further his education at Pennsylvania Military College and was a proud member of the Corps of Cadets. Upon graduation he went on active duty as a Lt. with the U.S. Marines on May 30, 1969.

Bob always had a great love for his country and below is a quotation from one of his last letters, sent as a message to some school children in the States:

"I take a great deal of pride in being a Marine serving over here so young kids like yourselves will be free to do as you choose and live in a free country, the greatest country in the world. Being younger than myself and living your whole life in the United States you do not realize how good you really have it. Most Americans take America for granted. I know I did until I came over here and saw how the rest of the people in the world live. Never be ashamed of the United States - it's the greatest - and always be proud of being an American."

****

ETERNAL FATHER, STRONG TO SAVE

Eternal Father, strong to save, Whose arm doth bind the restless wave, Who biddest the mighty ocean deep, Its own appointed limits keep: O hear us when we cry to Thee For those in peril on the sea.

O Trinity of love and power, Our brethren shield in danger's hour; From rock and tempest, fire and foe, Protect them wheresoe'er they go; And ever let there rise to Thee Glad hymns of praise from land and sea.

****

The God of peace, that brought again from the dead our Lord Jesus, that great Shepherd of the sheep, through the blood of the everlasting covenant, make you perfect in every good work to do His will, through Jesus Christ. Amen.

In solemn ceremonies at Holy Trinity Episcopal Church, Greenport, on Sunday, three Marines stood ceremonial guard, accompanied by a color guard from the Griswold-Terry-Glover Post Southold, consisting of Edward Grahoski, Dwain Horton, Curtis Horton and Russell E. Mann (above). Southold bade a hero's farewell to 1st Lieut. Robert H. Aldrich a helicopter pilot who was killed in action in Viet Nam on December 27, 1971. Below, the Aldrich family leaves the church, bearing the American flag.

This is from another service for Bob but unfortunately, there is no data either on the pictures or in the article.

THE VIRTUAL WALL ® VIETNAM VETERANS MEMORIAL www.VIRTUALWALL.org

Find A Name  The Virtual Wall® ▼ This Memorial Page ▼

Robert Henry Aldrich

First Lieutenant
HMM-165, 7TH FLEET
United States Marine Corps
Port Washington, New York
June 11, 1947 to December 27, 1971
ROBERT H ALDRICH is on the Wall at Panel W2, Line 131
See the full profile or name rubbing for Robert Aldrich

1LT ROBERT HENRY ALDRICH

THE VIRTUAL WALL ® VIETNAM VETERANS MEMORIAL www.VIRTUALWALL.org

Contact Us © Copyright 1997-2019 www.VirtualWall.org, Ltd ®(TM) Last update 09/12/2019

8/26/22, 12:59 PM www.VirtualWall.org Profile

Robert Henry Aldrich

ON THE WALL:	**Panel W2 Line 131**

This page Copyright© 1997-2018 www.VirtualWall.org Ltd.

PERSONAL DATA:	
Home of Record:	Port Washington, NY
Date of birth:	06/11/1947
MILITARY DATA:	
Service Branch:	United States Marine Corps
Grade at loss:	O2
Rank:	First Lieutenant
Promotion Note:	None
ID No:	102364656
MOS:	7562: PILOT HMH/M/L/A (I)
Length Service:	03
Unit:	HMM-165, 7TH FLEET
CASUALTY DATA:	
Start Tour:	Not Recorded
Incident Date:	12/27/1971
Casualty Date:	12/27/1971
Status Date:	Not Applicable
Status Change:	Not Applicable
Age at Loss:	24
Location:	Offshore, Indian Ocean
Remains:	Body not recovered
Repatriated:	Not Applicable
Identified:	Not Applicable
Casualty Type:	Non-hostile, died of other causes
Casualty Reason:	Helicopter - Pilot
Casualty Detail:	Air loss or crash at sea

URL: https:/www.VirtualWall.org/da/AldrichRH01a.htm

Data accessed: 8/26/2022

THE VIRTUAL WALL ® www.VirtualWall.org

Print This Page Close This Page

Page template 10/09/2015

https://www.virtualwall.org/js/Profile.htm

CHAPTER 4: ROBERT NORRIS CHINQUINA

Bob was a member of the PMC Class of 1969...see his Senior picture above. Bob won the Lt. William I Wolfgram Memorial Award in his Junior Year. He was also a Distinguished Military Student and ROTC Scholarship recipient in his Junior and Senior years. He received S.A.M.E. Service Award and won the Greater Philadelphia Rifle League Outstanding Performance Award. He was also a member of the Armor and Artillery Clubs and all four years was a member of the Rifle Team at PMC.

Robert and Ramona on their wedding day – June 1, 1970

Military Sabre Arch composed with the following PMC guests: Douglas Haywood, Francis (Teddy) Lotz, Lou Ogus, Lou Symanski, Tom Childers, Dennis (Erik) Bolton, Robert Aldrich, George Mueller

Bob grew up in Pimlico, right outside of Baltimore, MD, and was the son of Mr. and Mrs. Joseph Chinquina. He entered PMC in the summer of 1965 as a Rook. On January 21, 2023, I finally had the opportunity to speak to his widow Ramona about their relationship and Robert's activities prior to going to Vietnam. Robert and Ramona met in 1966 at the Howard Uniform Company where she was working. Robert worked there during the summer. They dated for three years and on June 1, 1969, they were married at St. Georges Episcopal Church in Dundalk, MD. In three consecutive days, Robert graduated, was commissioned as a Second Lieutenant in the Armor Branch, and they got married...busy times. In their wedding party were the following PMC Cadets: Doug Haywood, Lou Szymanski, Ted Lotz, Bob Aldrich, Tom Childers, George Mueller and Dennis (now known as Erik) Bolton.

For as long as she can remember, Robert wanted to make the Army his career. To put it Ramona's own words, that was "a given." She thought military life would be adventurous and fun. Robert's first assignment was at Ft. Knox, Kentucky. He went to the base while Ramona closed things up at their apartment and then joined him two weeks later or around July 4, 1969. Bob completed his training at Ft. Knox and then was assigned to Fort Benning, GA, for Ranger Training.

While at Fort Benning, Robert sprained his ankle on the obstacle course. He returned to Ft. Knox on May 10, 1970. On the next day, Ramona gave birth to their son, Robert Jr. Robert Sr. left for Vietnam on June 10, 1970. He only had one month with his newborn son.

Ramona said Robert Sr. was a supporting and loving husband. She loved to sew, so Robert bought her a sewing machine. He told her he didn't want her to work and they'd make ends meet on his salary. Since his career meant he would be away a lot, Ramona developed an attitude of independence. One of the requests Robert Sr. had discussed with Ramona, was to be buried at Arlington should he be killed in Vietnam. Ramona fulfilled all his requests except for this one.

This is a photo when Robert Jr. was one month old, just before Robert Sr. left for Vietnam...the last time he saw Ramona and Robert Jr.

*** All pictures courtesy of Ramona Chinquina

Robert leaning against the vehicle.

Robert wearing the helmet on an APC.

Robert relaxing in compound.

L-R- Doug Haywood, George Mueller and Robert Chinquina

In a *Philadelphia Inquirer* article dated August 16, 1970, Robert wrote a letter to Dean Sophocles, a professor and friend at PMC about his marriage:

> My wife has made me so very happy, and I miss her very much. We've been very lucky so far, and I've had all in my marriage that a man can ask for.

This letter was written right before his tragic death.

According to a letter written by Hal C. Pattison, Brigadier General USA (RET), President, The United States Armor Association, stated: "It was his deep sense of patriotism that prompted him (Robert) to volunteer for service in Vietnam."

Let's now go to Vietnam and follow Robert's actions in country. Robert arrived in Vietnam on June 15, 1970, in Bien Hoa Province and was assigned to B Troop, 1st Squadron, 11th Armored Cavalry Regiment. He was an Armored Reconnaissance Unit Commander. Not much is known of the details of his death aside from what appeared on The Blackhorse Memorial:

> Robert Norris Chinquina was killed while a passenger on a military vehicle on a mission when the weapon of another vehicle was accidentally discharged, striking [the] vehicle. Platoon leader and passenger on tank moving out of night defensive position. Another tank accidentally fired its main gun hitting this tank and another tank.

General Pattison also stated: "His presence there was typically Robert, for when his death came, he was in command, at the helm of his platoon, in his armored cavalry command track vehicle, moving to fulfill his responsibility and duty as a platoon leader."

Four Blackhorse troopers died in this incident:

- SP4 George Fredrick Beeler
- 1 Lt. Robert Norris Chinquina
- PFC Dickie Carson Curry
- PFC Timothy Allen White

I was fortunate enough to contact Doug Haywood, a PMC Classmate of Robert's, a friend and a fellow Army officer serving in Vietnam at the same time. Doug was an Infantry Officer, First Lieutenant, assigned to the 11th cavalry as an Aero Rifle Platoon Air Cav based out of Dian Base Camp...a couple of miles North of Saigon. Under his command were 32 troops whose primary mission was to recover crews from downed choppers, but they spent most of their time doing reconnaissance. Robert was an armored cavalry platoon leader with three Sheridan M551 tanks and six Armored Cavalry Assault Vehicles (APC) that were well armed with 50 caliber machine guns on either side. Doug was about a klick (1,000 meters/ 0.6214 mile/ 3,280.84 feet) away from Robert when the accident occurred.

Doug heard the weapon go off and then heard over the radio that the Platoon Leader of B troop was killed. He knew it was Robert.

Doug couldn't get to the site of the accident because he was leading his men on an assault mission. Doug learned that Robert was in a night defensive position and was going out on a reconnaissance mission. A tank from another platoon turned and accidentally fired its loaded 152mm main gun due to static electricity inside the tank. The shell hit Robert's vehicle and killed the four men in the vehicle.

Doug Haywood and Robert were close friends their Senior Year at PMC. They were both Company Commanders in the Corps and used to harass each other about Robert being a Tanker and Doug being a grunt or infantry man. In their senior year, they were together every day all the time. Doug described Robert as having a dry sense of humor who could be hilarious at times. He said Robert was very professional, didn't like BS, took care of his people. In his senior year, Robert read the tech manual on the M-60 Tank, so he could be technically proficient. One of the things that meant a lot to Doug was Robert's commitment to their friendship. When Doug was married only two weeks after Robert's son, was born, Robert drove from Baltimore, MD. to Collegeville., PA., to attend the ceremony and reception and then returned home all in one day. To Doug, that was a true friend and a great guy.

A few of his classmates have shared their thoughts about Bob while at PMC. Jim Pierson, "Spike," said he and Bob were friends during their time at PMC. Spike remembers Bob as a very bright guy who he had a quiet/subtle/wry sense of humor. Spike said Bob loved the military and looked forward to serving. Jim Hogg another of Bob's classmates and the Brigade Commander their Senior Year, commented that Bob was an outstanding officer.

Robert's body was escorted home by 1st Lt. Gerry Mc Swiggans. Gerry had his orders changed so he could be in charge of the funeral detail. Robert's viewing and services were on August 8, 1970, and were held at the Ruck Funeral Home in Baltimore, MD. At the service were members of Robert's family, Ramona and Robert, Jr., his parents, Mr. & Mrs. Joseph Chinquina, an honor guard, the PMC Commandant, Colonel Ford Fuller and his wife, members of the PMC Corps of Cadets, and friends. Robert was interred at the Gardens of Faith Cemetery, in Rosedale, MD, with full military honors and a twenty-one gun salute.

In the time that followed after Robert's death, he was recognized for his outstanding accomplishments as a PMC Cadet, an Armor Officer, a leader and a fantastic individual. Here are a few of honors bestowed on Robert after his passing.

In the picture below, which appeared in the PMC alumni magazine, *Impact*, Robert's widow, Ramona Chinquina, accepts a saber from Brig. General Hal Pattison (U.S. Army Ret.), President, The United States Armor Association, for Robert's selection for an award of "Outstanding Young Officer in the Army Branch" prior to his death. There were over 100 candidates.

Mrs. Ramona Chinquina, widow of Lt. Robert Chinquina '69, accepts **Armor** Association sabre from Brig. Gen. Hal Pattison (U. S. Army ret.), president of the association. Lieutenant Chinquina's parents, Mr. and Mrs. Joseph Chinquina, look on. Lieutenant Chinquina was named a winner of the award as an outstanding young officer in the Armor Branch shortly after he was killed in Vietnam in July.

The Blackhorse Memorial, which is dedicated to the fallen Troopers of the 11th Armored Cavalry Regiment, 1st Lt. Robert N. Chinquina (and the three other men who died with him) are all recognized and honored for their service.

Bronze Star Presented Posthumously To Lt.

GIVEN TO FAMILY -- The Bronze Star was presented posthumously to First Lieutenant Robert N. Chinquina, son of Mr. and Mrs. Joseph G. Chinquina of Nadine Drive for outstanding meritorious service in Vietnam. The award was presented to the lieutenant's wife, Mrs. Ramona G. Chinquina of Lange Street (center) by Col. Charles D. Decker, Jr., Fort Holabird Post Commander.

The family established a scholarship and medal in Robert's honor for future PMC students. The original award was a medal called the Pennsylvania Military College Lt. Robert N. Chinquina Memorial Award. After years of wear and tear, consideration is being given to changing it to an acrylic award called the CHINQUINA AWARD, presented to a Cadet for outstanding military merit in all activities of Alpha Company (Widener), Dauntless Battalion.

PENNSYLVANIA MILITARY COLLEGE
LT. ROBERT N. CHINQUINA
MEMORIAL AWARD
1947-1970
CHINQUINA AWARD
April 19, 2022
Presented to
For outstanding military
merit in all activities of
Alpha Company,
Dauntless Battalion.

Ramona thinks this is one of the last photos she received from Robert in Vietnam. She feels it was taken not long before he died. "In all the time we were together his hair was never this long. It was always cut military style. And I'd only seen a little mustache."

THE VIRTUAL WALL ® VIETNAM VETERANS MEMORIAL www.VIRTUALWALL.org

Find A Name ▼ | The Virtual Wall® ▼ | This Memorial Page ▼

Robert Norris Chinquina

First Lieutenant
B TRP, 1ST SQDN, 11TH ARMORED CAVALRY, USARV
Army of the United States
Baltimore, Maryland
February 18, 1947 to July 28, 1970
ROBERT N CHINQUINA is on the Wall at Panel W8, Line 61
See the full profile or name rubbing for Robert Chinquina

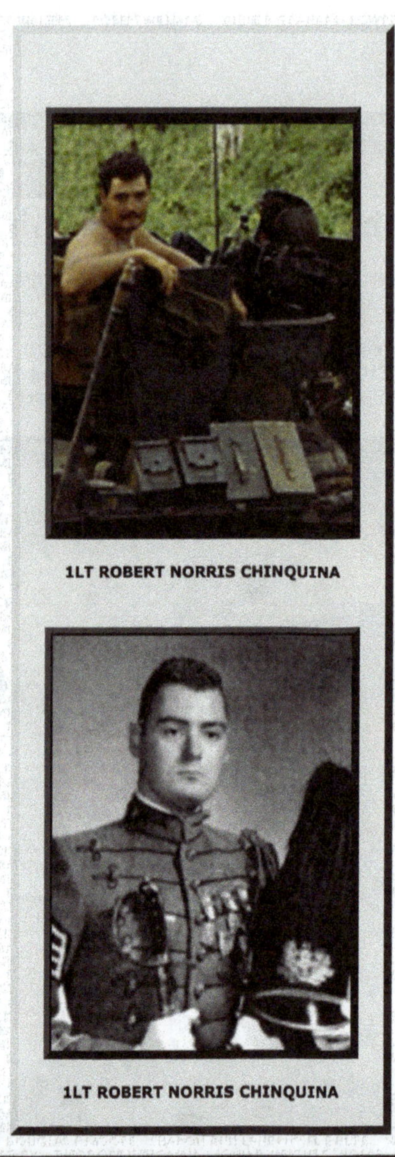

1LT ROBERT NORRIS CHINQUINA

1LT ROBERT NORRIS CHINQUINA

THE VIRTUAL WALL ® VIETNAM VETERANS MEMORIAL www.VIRTUALWALL.org

Contact Us © Copyright 1997-2019 www.VirtualWall.org, Ltd ®(TM) Last update 08/15/2019

December 2, 1970 CONGRESSIONAL RECORD — *Extensions of Remarks* E 10003

rejecting the House provisions will deprive many Americans of a reasonable opportunity to become investors in the free enterprise system.

In the area of performance fees, the conference committee eliminated the provisions of the House bill which would have exempted American investment advisers of offshore, or foreign based funds, from the restrictions on performance fees that will now apply to U.S. mutual fund advisers. Performance fees are commonplace throughout American business. Every salesman who works on a commission basis is paid a percentage of the results he achieves. The contingent fee, based on performance, is a fundamental business incentive and is one of the great engines that motivates the free enterprise system. It is important to the U.S. securities industry that foreign investors be encouraged to purchase American mutual funds and the securities of American companies. This not only gives depth, liquidity and continuity to U.S. securities markets, but has an important effect on reducing the balance-of-payments deficit.

In yet another area, the Conference Committee rejected the House bill provision that would allow fund holding companies to have the same total sales load as the other mutual funds with which they compete. Under the Senate bill, the sales load will be limited to 1½ percent. This is not only unfair discrimination, but a case of Federal price fixing, unjustified by any evidence in the record before our subcommittee.

All of these considerations suggest to me that the Conference Committee simply did not take into account the vastly changed economic conditions that prevail in the securities markets today. In the House we had the advantage of a much closer relationship to events than existed in the Senate in May 1969, when they considered this legislation. I believe the Conference Committee made a serious mistake, and I for one would not have voted for the bill had I known that this would be the ultimate result. I believe S. 2224 in its present form is regressive, antismall business, antisalesman, and antimiddle American investor. I would have hoped that we would strengthen the industry, increase investor protection, and make it possible for millions of more Americans to become equity participants in U.S. business. I am afraid S. 2224 turns back the clock and will limit these opportunities to the well-to-do, will stifle the growth in the number of shareholders in the United States, and will freeze the development of mutual funds.

1ST LT. ROBERT CHINQUINA

HON. CLARENCE D. LONG

OF MARYLAND

IN THE HOUSE OF REPRESENTATIVES

Wednesday, December 2, 1970

Mr. LONG of Maryland. Mr. Speaker, on July 23, 1970, 1st Lt. Robert Chinquina, of the 11th Armored Cavalry Division, was killed in Vietnam. In addition to his parents, Mr. and Mrs. Joseph Chinquina, he is survived by his wife, Ramona Vallerdi Chinquina, and his infant son, Robert, Jr. Lieutenant Chinquina was a graduate of the Pennsylvania Military College in Chester, Pa.

On November 5 of this year, Lieutenant Chinquina was posthumously commended and given an award by General Patterson (Ret.) on behalf of Armor Magazine for being one of the two most outstanding lieutenants commissioned from ROTC units or military colleges in the United States into the armored branch. Mrs. Chinquina received the award in her husband's name.

I should like to honor the memory of this young soldier by including this in the RECORD.

WASHINGTON'S BUILT-IN DESTABILIZERS

HON. JEFFERY COHELAN

OF CALIFORNIA

IN THE HOUSE OF REPRESENTATIVES

Wednesday, December 2, 1970

Mr. COHELAN. Mr. Speaker, the pressing problems of inflation and unemployment continue to cause untold hardships upon untold numbers of Americans. I have taken a strong stand against the Nixon administration's efforts and nonefforts in handling these problems.

Recently Dr. Virgil Salera, a former senior staff member of the Council of Economic Advisers, wrote an article on the inflation problem. I feel that it is most important that all Members of this Chamber and the readers of the RECORD to be fully aware of the alternative views on this issue. At this point, Mr. Speaker, I insert in the RECORD Dr. Salera's article, "Washington's Built-In Destabilizers," and I commend the reading of this article to my colleagues:

WASHINGTON'S BUILT-IN DESTABILIZERS

(By Virgil Salera)

There's a new way to focus on the question whether Washington's so-called stabilization role is worth as much as it costs. While we've been taught that some transfer payments and taxes provide modest built-in stabilizers, we haven't paid attention to the Government's own powerful built-in destabilizers. In particular, the neglect of Washington's adverse impact on productivity—that is, output per man-hour worked—has been nearly disastrous. It's time we developed an awareness that growth of productivity is unpredictable, and yet not autonomously cyclical.

For nearly 40 years Washington has believed that it alone controlled all the key levers for stabilizing a dynamic economy. Specifically, it thought it was fortunate to be able to count on increased aggregate spending to result in greater employment without inflation. The concurring view of most of the academic community was a powerful assist. Nearly everybody agreed that growing output per man-hour would prevent augmented total spending from markedly boosting prices and causing distortions in the economy.

CYCLICAL RISE

But what if productivity moved in jerky fashion, up in some periods and down in others—while yet conforming to a secular rise of some 3% a year? Then, our ability to attain and sustain economy-wide stability would depend on a complex and as yet little-understood relationship. Stability would depend on whether Washington could adjust the policy instruments within its control—fiscal and monetary—so that Government-induced changes in aggregate demand would dovetail with unstable short-term productivity developments which, once unleashed by excessive demand, were outside Washington's control.

The complexity of the dovetailing process is indicated in part by the conditions under which Washington does and does not influence the short-term rate of productivity. Surely Washington is virtually without influence when the nation's aggregate demand has remained for some years safely below inflationary levels. It is only when Washington flirts with serious inflation that the Government's own policies set in motion productivity-lowering forces over which there is no central control.

It will be noted that all this is a far cry from the usual reassuring views about the safely dependable long-term sources of productivity growth: The gradual improvement of labor skills, increased capital per head, and more or less steady assets on the technological front. It was not until these forces took off about two centuries ago that mankind in most Western countries was able to free itself from virtual stagnation.

Growth admittedly has created new problems of major scope. "Quality-of-life" issues readily come to mind. We don't, however, want to meet such challenges by way of returning to a stagnating situation. Thus, we have to be sure that we can cope successfully with stability requirements. The outlook would be more reassuring if the totality of Government operations exhibited sufficient flexibility.

The substantial difficulties Washington is likely to face from here on stem largely from habits of aggregate demand management coupled with the size and momentum of the programs that pressure groups now ask the national Government to finance. Most taxpayers are painfully aware that expenditures follow an expansionism all their own. The thousands of Washington spending programs are ratchet-governed: Operations move along a one-way street—upward and outward.

We've shaped an enormous machine that lacks a reverse gear. Imagine the reactions of constituents to legislators who, at a time of nose-diving productivity, insisted that the right thing was to vote for "reverse gifts"—fewer "free" benefits.

Our analysis need not proceed on the purely hypothetical level. Its significance is well illustrated in terms of Lyndon Johnson's record budget deficit of fiscal 1968 and its lingering repercussions. Skyrocketing Government outlays were occurring just as productivity was diving. There was not a peep out of Washington about the productivity aspect of the situation. The "guidelines" had been quietly abandoned in 1966, and less formal White House "jawboning" had taken their place. Washington thought it could meet major companies, and talk them out of proposed price increases despite strong inflationary pressures. Business volume was high, so why shouldn't price moderation reflect assumed "economies" of production at high rates of capacity utilization? Actually, workers were getting more dollars but producing less per dollar. Productivity was in steep decline. Washington, not labor, was at fault, since it had made the fatal mistake of overstimulating aggregate demand.

THREE NEGATIVE EFFECTS

The Government's easy spending on a lavish scale had neglected at least three adverse effects. The spending facilitated massive job-hopping, encouraged business firms to go for heavy overtime, and sharply curtailed the rate at which our economy weeded out inefficient managers. Job-hopping at an excessive pace makes for a notably wasteful rate of company recruiting, training and retraining, thus augmenting unit production costs that for a short period can easily be covered by raising product prices.

I asked Ramona, how she wanted people to remember Robert Sr.? She said, people used the following to describe him:

- Gentle and loving.
- Was a leader.
- Dedicated.
- Loyal.
- Hard worker.
- Loved the military.

I can't think of a better way to end this chapter than with following letter from Doug Haywood, PMC classmate, fellow officer, and most importantly, Robert's best friend.

Robert Jr., your dad was an outstanding man and human being, who loved his family and gave his life for his country doing what he loved to do. RIP Fellow Cadet and Vietnam Veteran Brother.

11th Armored Cavalry Regiment
APO San Francisco 96257

31 July 70

Dear Mona,

Joan and I send our deep, sincere sympathy to you and Bob Jr. Bob was a fine man and a fine officer. He was more dedicated than any other person, military or civilian, I have known. I think he and I became the best of friends while we were at the 11th Cav replacement school for seven days. I had decided, on the day that we were assigned to our units and reported to them, that Bob was the best friend that I had. Believe me, he still is.

Bob didn't suffer. I know this for a fact. He suffered no pain.

I spoke to some of his men out in the field while on a mission and they spoke so highly of him that I couldn't hope to convey his abilities and his character in words. He was highly thought of by his men.

He was a born leader

While he and I were having dinner at the club before we got assigned we both made an agreement. It was that if either of us should not return the other would do all he could to comfort the other's family. If there is anything — anything that Joan and I can possibly do, please confide in us. This was my last promise to your husband. He loved you so much. He spoke of you all the time and I'm sure that his last thoughts were of you. He was deeply and truly concerned and worried about you if anything happened to him. As I have said before, if there is anything we can do, (I will include a letter.) please ask.

Bob was a true friend. I feel now that he was my best friend. Especially when he came all the way from Maryland to attend our wedding. That is a friend. This is a great loss to me and I am truly sorry.

Sincere sympathy,
Doug Haywood.

8/26/22, 1:10 PM

www.VirtualWall.org Profile

Robert Norris Chinquina

ON THE WALL: **Panel W8 Line 61**

This page Copyright© 1997-2018 www.VirtualWall.org Ltd.

PERSONAL DATA:

Home of Record:	Baltimore, MD
Date of birth:	02/18/1947

MILITARY DATA:

Service Branch:	Army of the United States
Grade at loss:	02
Rank:	First Lieutenant
Promotion Note:	None
ID No:	212489035
MOS:	1204: Armored Reconnaissance Unit Commander
Length Service:	**
Unit:	B TRP, 1ST SQDN, 11TH ARMORED CAVALRY, USARV

CASUALTY DATA:

Start Tour:	06/15/1970
Incident Date:	07/28/1970
Casualty Date:	07/28/1970
Status Date:	Not Applicable
Status Change:	Not Applicable
Age at Loss:	23
Location:	Bien Hoa Province, South Vietnam
Remains:	Body recovered
Repatriated:	Not Applicable
Identified:	Not Applicable
Casualty Type:	Non-hostile, died of other causes
Casualty Reason:	Ground casualty
Casualty Detail:	Other accident
URL:	https://www.VirtualWall.org/dc/ChinquinaRN01a.htm
Data accessed:	8/26/2022

THE VIRTUAL WALL ® www.VirtualWall.org

Print This Page | Close This Page

Page template 10/09/2015

https://www.virtualwall.org/js/Profile.htm

CHAPTER 5: JOHN (JACK) LANCE GEOGHEGAN

Jack's Senior picture from the Class of 1963 yearbook.

Jack was the only child of John J. and Camille D. Geoghegan of Pelham Manor, New York. Jack arrived at Pennsylvania Military College as a member of the Class of 1963. Those who were the closest to him called him Jack. During his four years at PMC, he majored in English and was very active in both his Cadet and academic life. He was a member of Theta Chi Fraternity, Pershing Rifles, the Newman Club, and President of his Junior and Senior Classes, Reserved Officers Association, and the Student National Education Association. He enjoyed running track. However, of all his accomplishments at PMC, being selected as the Brigade Commander or First Captain his Senior Year was the most significant.

A few of Jack's closest friends during his four years at PMC wanted to share their thoughts about Jack. John Dishaw, who was also an English major and had the same classes for all four years, roomed in Howell Hall with Jack for two years and even spent some weekends with his friend in Pelham Manor. John was impressed that Jack shaved three times every morning to get ready for formation – never had a shadow. Jack was totally dedicated to the military. Jack was a wonderful athlete. When John asked about playing football, Jack declined because he wanted to focus on being the "number one Cadet." In their senior year, Jack was the Brigade Commander and received numerous leadership awards, among them the Bronze Cross for Achievement by the Army and the Navy Legion of Valor for the USA. John Dishaw described Jack as a "unique person." Jack was one of John's closest friends at PMC and part of John's wedding party after graduation. Unfortunately, John never saw Jack again.

John Stoeffler, another of Jack's Classmates and his roomie their junior year, describes Jack as a "great guy and good friend."

Dave McNulty, another of Jack's classmates and close friends, said they were both English majors, studied together, and were fraternity brothers in the sense of the word. Jack was a Theta Chi Brother but Dave was a "social brother" who hung around with Jack and John Dishaw. Dave and Jack were class officers. Jack was President and Dave was Secretary and both were Distinguished Military Students. Dave remembers Jack as a man of faith. Jack was a Catholic and every Sunday, even as the Brigade Commander, he marched the Catholic Cadets to church. Jack was gentle and kind, a man of character and leadership. Dave worked closely with Jack's widow and with director Randall Wallace on the film *We Were Soldiers*. More about that later.

My research assistant uncovered some impressive information about Jack in the Wolfgram Library at Widener University. In addition, Cammie, Jack's daughter, provided a lot of documents and photos. Unfortunately, her mom and Jack's wife and widow, Barbara, passed away on October 20, 2021, at the age of 79. Luckily, she passed a lot of her albums to Cammie. Barbara also left an outstanding summary of her life with Jack on the Virtual Wall about their life together, his death, the movie, and Barbara's life after Jack's death.

When I arrived at PMC as a Rook in 1964, I heard stories about Jack and believe me, those stories were not exaggerated. Prior to getting into his life after graduation, I think the reader needs to get a better understanding of Jack Geoghegan, the man, the Cadet, and the human being. He has to be one of the top cadets of the long gray line ever to have graduated from PMC.

It is difficult to find a starting point in talking about Jack while at PMC. However, I think one of his proudest moments was the visit to PMC by former President of the United States and the Supreme Allied Commander of the Allied Expeditionary Force during World War II, Dwight D. Eisenhower on May 31, 1963. It is my understanding that President Eisenhower's visit was the result of an invitation to visit PMC from Brigade Commander Jack Geoghegan.

On his visit to the PMC campus, President Eisenhower was presented with a saber by Brigade Commander Geoghegan.

The following pictures show President Eisenhower (escorted by Brigade Commander Jack Geoghegan) during his review of the Corps and the presentation of the saber.

President Dwight D. Eisenhower being escorted by Brigade Commander Jack Geoghegan.

President Eisenhower reviewed The Corps, was presented a sabre and received a plaque recognizing him as Honorary Cadet First Captain of the PMC Corps of Cadets.

The saber presented to President Eisenhower is in the archives collection at the Eisenhower Presidential Library in Abilene, KS.

Rather than trying to list all of Jack's accomplishments in academia, military (leadership), and in the community, I decided to rank a *few* of them. The list is not inclusive of everything Jack did; he was a unique person with extraordinary talents:

- Brigade Commander as a First Classman.
- Distinguished Military Student (see attached list).
- A letter from PMC President Moll for Jack's efforts to get the Corps to donate money for a Cadet's tuition so he could continue at PMC.
- The Legion of Valor Award (selected from 33 colleges). Jack was awarded the Bronze Cross for Achievement by the Army and Navy Legion of Valor of the United States of America.
- Brigade Commander who escorted General Shu-Ming Wang, head of the military staff committee of the United Nations, on his visit to PMC and review of the Corps of Cadets.

Jack was a busy person as the Brigade Commander but still had time for a social life. Barbara Weathers, the future Mrs. Jack Geoghegan, remembers October 7, 1962, when she attended a parade with a "very handsome red-haired cadet" in his dress uniform: Jack. He was the perfect gentleman and sat her in the stands with some other Cadets' girlfriends. When the Corps marched on the field, they all looked alike so she asked one of the girls, "Where is Jack?" The girl replied, "He's leading the parade." Barbara was shocked. He was the Brigade Commander and had never said a thing about it. As Barbara said, "That was just the beginning."

They started dating regularly. Barbara was amazed at his modesty, thoughtfulness, concern of others, and his humility and kindness. Jack graduated in June 1963. They were very much in love. They had discussed marriage but Jack received a two-year deferment from the Army to pursue other goals and Barbara was a senior at Beaver College. They waited until Barbara graduated from Beaver (now Arcadia University) in Glenside, PA . A week later they got married on June 13, 1964. They got married in a church near Beaver even though Barbara was from New Jersey. She chose the church because she had spent a lot of time there studying to become a Roman Catholic. They went to Bermuda for their honeymoon and then moved to a small apartment in Pelham,... close to Jack's parents.

DISTINGUISHED MILITARY STUDENTS

Alloway, George Dewey
Bell, Clarence Deshong, Jr.
Buccino, James Robert, Jr.
Chein, Kenneth
Clements, Gerald Charles
Dishaw, John David
Donchez, Alan Louis
Evonsky, William, II
Geoghegan, John Lance
Hallam, William Handley, II
Hansen, Albert, II
Hastings, Raymond Lloyd
Higgins, Richard Keyes
Huber, John Joseph
Kissinger, Stuart Henry, III
Lenhart, Michael Eugene, Jr.
Long, Samuel Gabrial, Jr.
McNulty, David Wayne
Melin, Jeffrey Nicholas
Miller, William Glen
Nadig, Carroll Craig
Overton, Bruce Bird
Plaxe, Jack Roger
Schenke, Rodger Stephen
Carl P. Sparano
Tilelli, John Harold
Urban, Gerald Gregory
Zeltner, Richard Lemmon

Twenty-eight Cadets were presented Distingusihed Military Student Awards in two separate reviews held at Pennsylvania Military College. Making the presentations on Sunday, November 4th, was Major General Raymond Bell, Deputy Commanding General, Second United States Army, Fort George Meade, Maryland. The presentations were made on Sunday, November 11, by Major General James C. Frank, Commanding General of the 79th Infantry Division, Harrisburg, Pennsylvania.

PENNSYLVANIA MILITARY COLLEGE
OFFICE OF THE PRESIDENT
CHESTER, PENNSYLVANIA

2 October 1961

Mr. John L. Geoghegan, President
Junior Class
Pennsylvania Military College
Chester, Pa.

Dear Jack:

The Class of 1963 has achieved a unity and an understanding of the problems of its classmates that has, to my knowledge, never before been demonstrated at Pennsylvania Military College. I believe that your accomplishments in collecting funds for the tuition of a classmate whose continuance at college was in jeopardy is unprecedented in any institution, and could have occurred at no other place than P.M.C. This in itself - more than any other thing - characterizes the cohesion of a cadet corps and the values of this type of living.

Each of us in the administration is overjoyed by the initiative that you have exercised and the leadership which you have displayed.

Please accept this small addition to your efforts.

Sincerely yours,

Clarence R. Moll

(Dictated on Friday - 29 September - but not typed until today)

Alumni Bulletin January 1963

Geoghegan Receives Legion of Valor Award

CADET BRIGADE COMMANDER SELECTED FROM 33 COLLEGES:

Mr. J. Whiting Friel and Cadet Geoghegan

Cadet Captain John L. Geoghegan, Brigade Commander, has been awarded the Bronze Cross for Achievement by the Army and Navy Legion of Valor of the United States of America.

This selection represents the second consecutive year this coveted award has been granted to a PMC cadet. Last year Cadet Robert Bellinger was the recipient.

The award, made annually by the Legion of Valor, is based on Cadet Captain Geoghegan's having been chosen the outstanding Junior Class Cadet in the XXI

U. S. Army Corps area during the 1961-62 academic year. This area embraces the States of Pennsylvania, Maryland, Delaware, Virginia, and the District of Columbia, and contains 33 Colleges and Universities which offer the Army ROTC program.

To perpetuate the ideals of patriotism and loyalty, the Army and Navy Legion of Valor, which ranks as one of the oldest veterans' organizations in the United States, was originally formed by a group of men who had been awarded the Medal of Honor in the Civil War or the Indian Campaigns. In 1918, it admitted to membership recipients of the Army's Distinguished Service Cross; and in 1933, those who had received the Navy Cross were permitted to join.

Geoghegan and two young admirers.

Representing the Legion of Valor at the review, and presenting the award, was Mr. J. Whiting Friel, of Jenkintown, Pennsylvania.

In the First World War, Mr. Friel was awarded the Distinguished Service Cross for swimming the Schelch River in Belgium with two other men while in full view of the enemy and under heavy artillery and machine gun fire and assisting in the construction of a foot bridge which materially aided in the successful operation of American troops in the vicinity. The two men with Mr. Friel were killed during the action. Among his other decorations are the Silver Star, Purple Heart, French Croix de Guerre with 2 Palms and the Belgian Croix de Guerre.

Dr. Clarence R. Moll, president of the college, stated, "The selection of Cadet Captain Geoghegan for this award not only brings well-merited recognition of his outstanding record as a student and cadet, but also reflects most favorably on PMC and its ROTC program."

ALUMNI BULLETIN • JANUARY, 1963

27
a

GENERAL WANG REVIEWS THE CORPS

General Shu-Ming Wang, head of the military staff committee of the United Nations, reviews the Corps of Cadets and honor guard during homecoming weekend. Gen. Wang is shown being escorted by Cadet Geoghegan and General Biddle.

Jack spent the first year after graduating from PMC at the University of Pennsylvania studying and receiving his Master's in International Relations. Barbara said Jack was getting restless and wanted to do something for people in need. He had searched out several options but they decided to work with Catholic Relief Services. In July 1964, they sublet their apartment and they left for Tanganyika (now Tanzania) in Africa. Jack ran a school lunch program that fed 120,000 children a day. In Barbara's own words, "The experience in Tanzania fulfilled his loving, altruistic, giving spirit."

When they returned to the US for Jack to begin his military commitment to the Army, they went to Fort Benning, GA for Jack's Infantry Officers Basic Course. Barbara became pregnant in Africa, and while at Ft. Benning, gave birth to their precious daughter, Camille Ann Geoghegan (named after her two grandmothers) on June 8,1965.

With his basic course completed, Jack was assigned to the 1st Battalion, 7th Cavalry, under the command of Lieutenant Colonel Harold (Hal) Moore – yes, the infamous military leader in Vietnam. (More later on LTC Moore.) Before leaving for Vietnam, Barbara, Jack, and Cammie visited his parents in Redding, CT. Jack was an only child and very close to his parents. Jack's father, according to Barbara, was full of grief and feared he would never see Jack again. This is not the first premonition like this has surfaced with some of these eight men's loved ones. Jack left for Vietnam on August 18, 1965.

Second Lieutenant Jack Geoghegan arrived in Vietnam on August 18, 1965. He was the Platoon Leader of the 2nd Platoon, C Company, 1st Battalion, 7th Cavalry, 1st Cav Division in their base camp in An Khe, South Vietnam, halfway between the coast and the Vietnam/Cambodia border. Jack began writing letters to Barbara and his parents about his units patrolling and manning the defensive perimeter. He felt his men were becoming more professional every day. Jack said, "Even Grand Central Station seems a paradise right now. Oh, how I will enjoy a quiet ride in Connecticut with no one shooting at me. Death is so close that the small things make life worthwhile – a cup of coffee, a drink of water. Please do not get me wrong. I'm not complaining, only thanking God for the opportunity to learn what is really important and to see what honor can be like. It will make me a much better man. We learn each day." Those who knew him would say, "That's Jack."

Jack and Barbara on their wedding day.

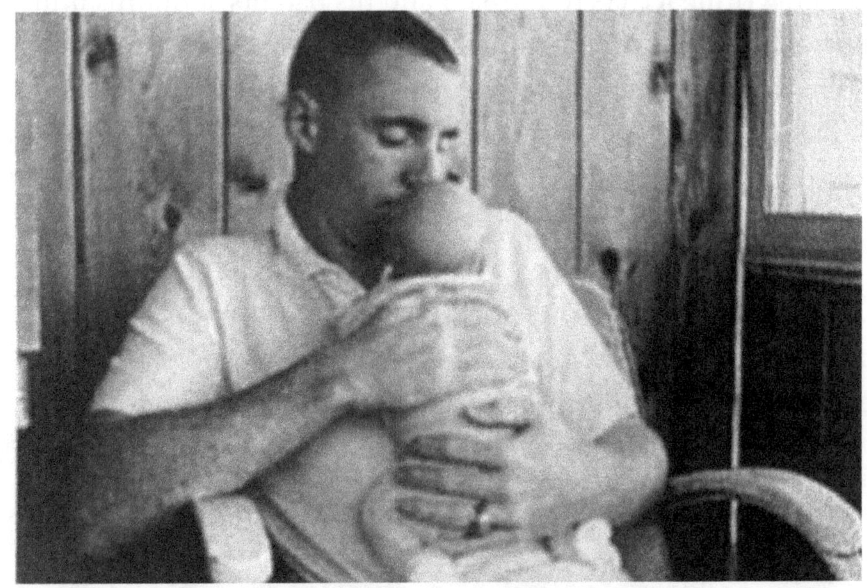

Jack with his daughter Cammie just before he left for Vietnam.

Barbara, Cammie, and Jack Geoghegan

On November 15, 1965, in la Drang Valley, "The Valley of Death" lived up to its reputation. Jack was part of a battalion of around 400 men who were attacked by an enemy force of 2,000 NVAs (North Vietnam Army) dug into an interconnecting warren of mountainside tunnels. According to LTC Moore. Jack was in a fox hole directing his men when he heard cries for help. The enemy small arms fire was intense but he saw SP4 Willie Godboldt, wounded and in need of help. A sergeant in the fox hole said he'd go, but Lt. Geoghegan went. As he reached Willie, Lt. Geoghegan was shot in the back and his head. In a letter later mailed to Barbara, Lt. Devney, B Company, 1st Bn, 7th Cav., who served with Jack in Vietnam, said Jack was a good friend and a good officer – a well-respected platoon leader in the battalion. In Lt. Devney's words, "Jack did not suffer at all. Actually he never knew what hit him." According to an article written by David T. Zabecki, "Ghosts of la Drang," in the Vietnam magazine, December 2011, "Jack Geoghegan was among the first of 234 cavalrymen killed in the horrific combat at LZ's X-Ray and Albany in the la Drang Valley in November 1965."

In April of 2023, one of my Classmates, Colonel Tom Vossler, was awarded the John L. Goeghegan Alumni Citizenship Award. Accompanying Tom at the Awards Event was Colonel Bob Edwards, Jack Geoghegan's Company Commander in Vietnam (then a Captain) on the fateful day, 15 November 1965.

With Tom's help, I began to communicate with Colonel Edwards, a highly decorated, 23-year US Army career veteran, to discuss the battle at la Drang and Jack Geoghegan. Colonel Edwards sent me a 104-page document to help me to get a better understanding of what the Americans were up against and especially his Company C and the second platoon led by 2nd Lieutenant Goeghegan. Colonel Edwards wrote this document on 6 February 1967 during his Career Course, US Army Infantry School, Ft. Benning, GA. The document was entitled:

> Operations of the 1st Battalion, 7tn Cavalry, 1st Cav Division (Airmobile) in the Airmobile Assault of Landing Zone X-Ray, la Drang Valley, Republic of Viet Nam, 14-16 November 1965. (Personal Experience of a Company Commander.

The document is extremely well written with maps of the la Drang Valley, LZ locations, troop strength of the enemy (estimated), and the friendly troops, casualties, operations plans, evacuation plan, etc.

With Colonel Edwards' help, I will attempt to revisit the battle and its impact on the American soldiers and especially on Lt. Geoghegan. The estimated strength of all enemy forces on 14 Nov was 2,000 NVA. US forces committed on 14 Nov were a total of 430 officers and enlisted men. For the assault, three Landing Zones were evaluated and X-Ray was selected as the primary LZ. First to land was B Company whose job was to secure the LZ. Once that was completed, Company A, Company C, and Company D would follow.

Company B and A had encountered little resistance at the LZ. An enemy force of 175-200 was heading for the LZ. The enemy force was taken under fire by C Company and the enemy attack was halted. For the next hour and a half, C Co. fought the enemy in this sector and with the assistance of artillery and ARA (aerial rocket artillery provided by B Model Hueys that have a pod on each side with 38 2.75" rockets) fire and were able to defeat the attack. This was a significant accomplishment by C Company due to its being outnumbered and under heavy ground fire.

The next day on November 1965, at 0650 hours, the enemy launched a vicious attack on the C Co. sector with a force of two or three companies. At 0715 hours, C Company Commander, Captain Edwards, was wounded in his left shoulder/scapula by an enemy bullet after he threw a grenade at the approaching enemy. Despite his injury early in the fighting, he continued to command for three hours and requested reinforcements from the Battalion CO. At first, LTC Moore said no and ordered Capt. Edwards had to hold the area. Later, LTC Moore sent a platoon to support C Co. but the platoon encountered a series of savage encounters with the enemy and never reached C Company.

Here are the battle results:

- 1st Platoon Leader was found KIA (killed in action) with 5five dead enemies in and around his position.
- All C Co. officers were casualties by 0800 hours...2 KIA and three WIA (Wounded in action)...including the Company Commander.
- 42 soldiers KIA.

In the early, pre-Cobra days of aerial rocket artillery (ARA), the always paired rocket ship of the 2nd of the 20th were UH-1 Hueys (Photo provided by Colonel Bob Edwards).

When I asked Colonel Edwards to describe Jack Geoghegan he said, "He was level headed, always on top of the situation, very soldier oriented, genuinely concerned about their welfare and tactically proficient. He was a good officer and more mature then the average Second Lieutenant."

Jack's body was escorted home by his brother-in-law, Captain Paul Weathers, United States Marines. A military funeral was held at St. Catharine's Church, in Pelham, NY, on December 2, 1965. An honor guard from Pennsylvania Military College was present along with Major General William S. Biddle, Commandant of Cadets and Clarence R. Moll, President of Pennsylvania Military College. Jack was buried following the mass with full military honors at St. Mary's Cemetery in Bethel, CT.

Jack's passing brought accolades from multiple members of the PMC staff and administration:

- **Dr. Clarence R. Moll, President of PMC** – "Though physically removed he continues to live among us as the symbol of all that is right and good. His ideals continue to serve us as a standard for others to reach, his sincerity a measure of our own integrity, and his dedication the test of our own sense of honor and service."
- **Major General William S. Biddle, Commandant of Cadets** – "When, that summer, the time came to select a Brigade Commander for the ensuing year, there was no serious competition for the post: all concerned were agreed that it should go to John Geoghegan." General Biddle also said, "By any measure, he was one of Pennsylvania Military College's most promising sons."

In an article by **Carl R. Lobel Managing Editor**, *The Dome*, entitled "I Can Still Feel The Impact", December 2, 1965, came the following statements about Jack:

- **Bill Symolon, Brigade Commander** – "He was the finest leader that has come from PMC in my time, and was an inspiration to all who came in contact with him. Although I knew him from a distance, I can still feel the impact of his leadership upon me."
- **William J. Nelson, Class of '63** - "With all the responsibilities and duties, he took upon himself, he nonetheless always had time to give to those who needed him, regardless of class or rank. I feel it was this trait, more than any other, which won for Jack the admiration of all those who knew him."
- **Michael J. Hubbard, Captain, AGC** - "He was always giving of himself to others... a truly unselfish person."
- **Homer Nearing, Professor of English** - "Jack Geoghegan was one of the most versatile students PMC has had. Moreover, he had an exceptionally attractive personality. He represented the ideal of what PMC cadet program tries to achieve."
- **Wm. L Cottee , Dean of Student Personnel**, who said The Francis M. Taitt Award, which Jack received in May of 1963, described Jack so very well..."to an outstanding soldier and gentleman."
- **C. Arthur Littman, '60, Director of Alumni Relations**: Jack made the supreme sacrifice fighting for the ideals he cherished so dearly. Our alma mater has suffered a great loss. The entire alumni are

saddened and will long remember Jack Geoghegan and his devotion to PMC.

- **Harold G. Moore, Colonel, Infantry** (Jack's Battalion Commander in la Drang Valley), in a letter to Barbara dated 9 March 1966 – "Jack led his platoon in his last hours as always in a truly professional, valorous, and outstanding manner. His platoon was attacked by an enemy force which outnumbered his men but he never gave up an inch. He stood and fought and his men stood with him. They repelled and defeated the enemy attack. He met our God as a fighting leader completely true to his deep integrity."

Barbara stayed in Connecticut for four years and during that time, she and Jack's parents were visited by Colonel Hal Moore in 1967. Barbara stated:

> We had a wonderful, cathartic meeting with him at the Geoghegans' home that lasted five hours. He presented me with the Presidential Unit Citation ribbon that day. I will never forget as long as I live what his visit meant to us and how healing it was for us. We continued to hear from Colonel Moore every November, even as he rose in rank to three-star general with many more responsibilities.

In Connecticut through a mutual friend, Barbara met her second husband, John Johns, and they were married in late 1968 and then moved to West Point in NY where LTC Johns was stationed. He retired from the Army in 1978 as a Brigadier General.

In 1990, Barbara received a call from Joe Galloway. He asked her to contribute to a book he was writing with Hal Moore.

The chapter was about the families left behind. The book was entitled, *We Were Soldiers Once...and Young*, and it became a best seller. In 1998, General Moore let Barbara know she may receive a call from Randall Wallace who had bought the screen rights to the book. Randall Wallace wanted to tell Jack's story.

> Jack Geoghegan's story is one that I find to be especially important, in that it seems to me to be representative of the finest and best spirit among the young Americans who went to Vietnam – either physically, as the soldiers did, or spiritually, as families back home.

Barbara spent the next three weeks going through a trunk full of memorabilia dating back 40 years. She wrote an eight-page letter..."and the process of doing it filled my soul with a peace that gave my memory of Jack added solace and happiness...

Three years later, in March 2002, *We Were Soldiers* was released starring Mel Gibson as LTC Moore. Chris Klein played Jack Geoghegan, Keri Russell played Barbara Geoghegan and they even had an infant for their daughter, Cammie. The movie is 138 minutes long. Dave McNulty, Jack's close friend at PMC, contributed information to Randall Wallace about Jack and their friendship while at PMC. In Dave's words, the movie is, "the most authentic and realistic film on the Vietnam War ever made. The Army uses it as part of its officer infantry basic training." After watching it, I feel it shows the human side of a soldier...husband, father, brother, son, believer, team member, and leader, To all the men who died in la Drang in this battle... God Bless and Rest In Peace...you are not forgotten!

Jack Geoghegan has received numerous awards and recognition for his bravery, heroism and leadership:

- The Silver Star (see the Award and Citation enclosed).
- Ceremony Honoring PMC Alumni Killed in Vietnam (See pic enclosed).
- Bronze Star with V (Valor)
- By the Republic of South Vietnam: National Order, fifth class and the Gallantry Cross with Palm.
- Combat Infantry Badge or CIB.
- Presidential Unit Citation presented by Colonel Moore.
- The Purple Heart

At Widener University (formerly PMC), the University established two Alumni Awards in his honor:

- John L. Geoghegan Alumni Citizenship Award: This award is given in the memory of John L Geoghegan '63 to a graduate who has brought honor to the University through academic achievement, demonstrates leadership capabilities and community service.
- John L. Geoghegan Student Citizenship Award: This award is given in the memory of John L. Geoghegan '63 to a current student who has brought honor to the University through academic achievement, demonstrated leadership capabilities and community service.

I am sure there have been more awards given to Jack since he was killed in Vietnam but I have focused on only a few. Jack was a man of great faith, deep integrity, outstanding leadership ability, remarkable character, and high moral standards. He cared more about his men than himself. He was a respected soldier, husband, father, and son – lost to the world at the young age of 24. RIP, Brother!

Probably the last picture taken of Jack on board a ship bound for Vietnam.

THE UNITED STATES OF AMERICA

TO ALL WHO SHALL SEE THESE PRESENTS, GREETING:

THIS IS TO CERTIFY THAT
THE PRESIDENT OF THE UNITED STATES OF AMERICA
AUTHORIZED BY ACT OF CONGRESS JULY 9, 1918
HAS AWARDED

THE SILVER STAR

TO
JOHN L. GEOGHEGAN
(THEN SECOND LIEUTENANT, UNITED STATES ARMY)
FOR
GALLANTRY IN ACTION
in the Republic of Vietnam on 15 November 1965

GIVEN UNDER MY HAND IN THE CITY OF WASHINGTON
THIS 6th DAY OF February 19 97

EARL M. SIMMS
BG, USA, THE ADJUTANT GENERAL

SECRETARY OF THE ARMY

The President of the United States of America, authorized by an Act of Congress, July 9, 1918, has awarded the Silver Star to

JOHN L. GEOGHEGAN
(THEN SECOND LIEUTENANT, UNITED STATES ARMY)

FOR GALLANTRY IN ACTION:

against a numerically superior force of North Vietnam Regulars on 15 November 1965 while assigned as Platoon Leader, 2d Platoon, Company C, 1st Battalion, 7th Cavalry, 1st Cavalry Division (Airmobile) in the Republic of Vietnam. When his company was attacked by a large enemy force, the weight of the attack fell on Lieutenant Geoghegan's platoon and the platoon on line to his right. Within minutes, the fighting became close-in and furious as the North Vietnamese attempted to overrun the American positions. Suddenly, one of Lieutenant Geoghegan's riflemen was wounded a few meters to his right and yelled for help. Without hesitation, Lieutenant Geoghegan rose from his foxhole command post and selflessly exposed himself to the sheets of enemy fire as he ran out to assist his wounded trooper, receiving fatal wounds in the process. Ultimately, his platoon held their ground and repelled the attack. Lieutenant Geoghegan's intrepid gallantry in action in voluntarily laying his own life on the line for love of one of his men was in keeping with the highest traditions of the military service and reflect great credit on himself, the 7th Cavalry Regiment, and the United States Army.

Ceremonies Honor Alumni Killed in Vietnam

At a ceremony in the Alumni Auditorium on Nov. 18 honoring four alumni killed in Vietnam, General James K. Woolnough, commanding general, U. S. Continental Army Command, unveils plaque provided by the Army in honor of Lt. John L. Geoghegan '63, killed in battle Nov. 15, 1965; Lt. William J. Stephenson '63, who fell in battle Feb. 23, 1966; and Capt. Daniel F. Monahan '62, killed April 14, 1967. Shown with Gen. Woolnough are, from left: Carol Stephenson, Betty Monaghan and Barbara Geoghegan.

THE VIRTUAL WALL ® VIETNAM VETERANS MEMORIAL www.VIRTUALWALL.org

Find A Name ▼ The Virtual Wall® ▼ This Memorial Page ▼

John Lance Geoghegan

Second Lieutenant

2ND PLT, C CO, 1ST BN, 7TH CAVALRY, 1ST CAV DIV, USARV

Army of the United States

New York, New York

November 10, 1941 to November 15, 1965

JOHN L GEOGHEGAN is on the Wall at Panel 3E, Line 56

See the full profile or name rubbing for John Geoghegan

Jack was the only child of John J. and Camille D. Geoghegan
First husband of Barbara Weathers Geoghegan Johns, married June 13, 1964
Father of Camille Ann Geoghegan Olson, born June 8, 1965
Grandfather of Stephanie Grace Olson, born March 11, 1997
and Julia Marie Olson, born October 30, 2000.

from Pelham, New York and
West Redding, Connecticut

Jack's life was one of great leadership and service to others, and that is how he died.

In an effort to save the life of one of his men in the Battle of the Ia Drang Valley, they were both killed.

The name of SP4 Willie Frank Godboldt, Jacksonville, Florida is next to Jack's on the Vietnam Veterans Memorial, panel 3 E, line 56.

A memorial from
Barbara Weathers Geoghegan Johns,
BJ2Johns@cs.com

Jack as Brigade Commander with former president Dwight D. Eisenhower at 1963 graduation weekend at Pennsylvania Military College.

Jack on board a ship bound for Vietnam with the First Air Cavalry Division, 1965.

8/24/22, 10:06 AM www.VirtualWall.org Profile

John Lance Geoghegan

ON THE WALL: **Panel 3E Line 56**

This page Copyright© 1997-2018 www.VirtualWall.org Ltd.

PERSONAL DATA:
Home of Record: New York, NY
Date of birth: 11/10/1941

MILITARY DATA:
Service Branch: Army of the United States
Grade at loss: O1
Rank: Second Lieutenant
Promotion Note: None
ID No: 05222616
MOS: 1542: Infantry Unit Commander
Length Service: 02
Unit: 2ND PLT, C CO, 1ST BN, 7TH CAVALRY, 1ST CAV DIV, USARV

CASUALTY DATA:
Start Tour: 08/18/1965
Incident Date: 11/15/1965
Casualty Date: 11/15/1965
Status Date: Not Applicable
Status Change: Not Applicable
Age at Loss: 24
Location: Pleiku Province, South Vietnam
Remains: Body recovered
Repatriated: Not Applicable
Identified: Not Applicable
Casualty Type: Hostile, died outright
Casualty Reason: Ground casualty
Casualty Detail: Gun or small arms fire
URL: www.VirtualWall.org/dg/GeogheganJL01a.htm
Data accessed: 8/24/2022

THE VIRTUAL WALL ® www.VirtualWall.org

Print This Page Close This Page

Page template 10/09/2015

www.virtualwall.org/js/Profile.htm

CHAPTER 6: DENNIS ROSS PAUL ISOM

Dennis grew up in Drexel Hill, Pennsylvania. He was the son of Mrs. Alice Isom of Upper Darby. A graduate of Upper Darby High School (1966) prior to attending Pennsylvania Military College as a member of the Class of 1966, Dennis was a Political Science major and a member of the Political Science Honor Society. He belonged to the Circle K, the Newman Club, the Chess Club, and the Ranger Platoon where he was selected as the Platoon Leader. He was also the Editor of *The Saber and Sash,* the PMC Yearbook. He was a Distinguished Military Student or DMS. Above is his Senior picture from his yearbook.

Dennis in his PMC Ranger uniform in 1966.

In his Senior year at PMC, Dennis' Brigade Commander (First Captain) was Bill Symolon. They had been friends their entire four years at PMC and Bill wanted to share his thoughts on Dennis. Bill said in their leadership classes, they were taught the ancient maxim from Plutarch and Alexander the Great: "An army of sheep led by a lion is more to be feared than an army of lions led by a sheep." Anyone who knew Dennis Isom from our Class of 1966 would see him embodied in the quotation. Bill described Dennis as a man of slight build, quiet demeanor, and fierce spirit. Dennis aimed at becoming a career Army officer and wanted to earn a regular commission upon graduation. Dennis quickly established himself as a highly motivated, truly dedicated soldier-in waiting. At PMC, the Ranger Platoon was established and led by Dennis, the Platoon Leader and the tactical officer, Captain Doug Detlie, a West Point graduate and Army Ranger. The Ranger Platoon had in-class training during the week along with physical fitness workouts and bivouacs on scheduled weekends. The group even aligned with a local sky diving group near campus and made their first jumps as cadets.

Bill shared an interesting story from their Junior year:

The Vietnam War was slowly building up and Dennis and I talked of dropping out of school to enlist so as not to miss the action. One day I met with Col. Noel A. Menard, our Commandant of Cadets, who was a superior leader and close mentor to many of our classmates. I told Col. Menard of our plan and when he asked me why we would want to leave school so early I told him, essentially, that Dennis and I were going to be career soldiers, he in the Army and myself in the Marines, that if there was a war on, career military men needed to be in it, didn't they? The Col. agreed with all of that, but then said the following to me: "It is true that professional soldiers need to be in the wars we fight, but the Army (and Marines) need lieutenants as badly as they need privates, in some cases we need them more. You should both finish school and earn your commissions. When you're lieutenants and the war is still on, you will both be sent there in short order. If the war is over by then, you won't have missed anything. It won't have been a war."' We knew that Col. Menard himself served in Vietnam as an advisor shortly before he retired and joined the staff at PMC. We held him in the highest regard and took his advice to heart."

PMC March 1966 General Throckmorton Honor Guard

Bill also shared a discussion he had with Dennis shortly before graduation. They knew they would probably be in Vietnam as Infantry officers. Dennis said, "Bill, when I get to Vietnam, I will come home a hero or I won't come home." Bill concluded, "Dennis did not come home from Vietnam. But, Dennis is a hero."

Dennis had the great fortune of being the Executive Officer (XO) for Bravo Company his Senior Year at PMC in August of 1965, specifically because of one particular Rook, Tom Dougherty. He introduced Dennis to his sister and future wife, Patricia, who was visiting PMC. The situation affected Tom in several ways. As Dennis and Patricia dated, Dennis went out of his way to make sure he wasn't giving Tom any undue favoritism or slack – just the opposite. Still, Tom felt Dennis was fair and very disciplined.

Patricia and Dennis, November 1965, PMC Dorm 5 Reception Room.

Dennis and Patricia dated and when she visited Dennis at PMC in Chester, PA, she would stay at a local hotel the name of which she cannot remember. They liked to eat at the Tres Bon Diner in Chester, PA. Patricia recalled one adventure when the hotel locked their doors at 9:00 pm one night Dennis had to climb up the side of the building to the window of her room to get to see her. She recalls having some wonderful adventures. "We were very, very young and didn't realize how fragile our time together was."

Dennis graduated and received his Regular Army commission from PMC in 1966. On June 10, 1966, he and Patricia were married at St. Michael's Catholic Church in Baltimore, MD. They honeymooned in Bermuda. When they returned to the US, Dennis' first duty assignment was at Indian Town Gap, PA, for training. His next assignment was to be stationed at Ft. Benning, GA, as a second lieutenant. In Patricia's words, "Our stay at Ft. Benning was a disaster." They arrived in the middle of a heat wave and none of the apartments had air conditioning, not even window units. From Ft. Benning, Dennis went to Korea in 1967 for a year. Upon his return to the US, Dennis was assigned to Ft. Jackson, South Carolina. Patricia joined him. She remembered the apartment they had off-base had "avocado" colored appliances. Tom Dougherty visited them at Ft. Jackson where he and Dennis would go fishing or out to dinner at the O (Officers) Club. Of course, Patricia would join them. While at Ft. Jackson, Dennis was promoted to Captain. They enjoyed the area with friends both in the neighborhood and on the base and they liked exploring the surrounding community. Dennis enjoyed playing the guitar. Some evenings they would get together with the neighbors and sing popular folk songs. Tom visited them before Dennis left for Vietnam. Dennis was ready but Tom thought he was apprehensive...a lot of soldiers were dying every day. Dennis and Patricia stayed at Ft. Jackson for a year before Dennis was sent to Vietnam.

Bridal Party- Flower girl Gina. Left to Right: Louise Laskin, Charlotte Eshleman and Pam Miles, Patricia and Dennis, John Hoke, Steve Mellish and Frank Platt.

Capt. Dennis Isom, Vietnam, February 1969.

Troops being resupplied by a CH-47 or Chinook in February 1969.

Dennis arrived in Vietnam on January 29, 1969, and was assigned to A Company, 3rd Battalion, 8th Infantry, 4th Infantry Division, as an Infantry Unit Commander, in Kontum Province, Central Highlands region. On March 3, 1969, in a place called the Plei Trap Valley just northwest of Pleiku, A Company, 3/8

Infantry 4th Infantry Div., commanded by Captain Dennis Isom was attacked a much larger force of the 66th North Vietnamese Army (NVA) regiment. In an article entitled "Ambush in Plei Trap Valley" written by John F. Bauer, platoon leader with D Company that appeared in the *VFW Magazine* in February 2008, " As the men made their way along a ridgeline, they killed two NVA soldiers, and that's when the firefight began. A machine gun opened up at close range, killing one soldier and wounding another." According to Bauer, Captain Isom learned of the engagement and rushed to reinforce the platoon with elements of A Company. Captain Isom immediately called for air support. Bauer reports, " At this time, Isom's RTO (Radio telephone operator) got hit trying to dash for cover, and when Captain Isom went to his aid, he was killed instantly by a burst of machine gun fire across the chest."

According to Bauer, 31% of the 86 (27) men in A Company lost their lives.

In his last letter to Patricia, Dennis said he felt confident in the job he was doing and safe as the Chaplain had given him communion in the field. Dennis was a devout Catholic. Initially, Patricia was notified that Dennis was missing in action and they had not recovered his body. When they did, it was three weeks later. The body went to a funeral home in Pennsylvania with instructions not to open the casket for her unless there was a doctor present. She opted not to have it opened so she could remember Dennis as he was when he left. When his body was returned Patricia was given his wedding ring and the plastic rosary from communion. In his obituary from *The Philadelphia Inquirer* on March 19, 1969, reported that Cadets from Pennsylvania Military College participated in a military funeral with full honors. The pallbearers, color guard, firing squad, buglers, and an honor guard were from The Corps of Cadets.

A solemn requiem mass was celebrated at St. Anastasia Church, Newtown Square, PA. Dennis was interred at SS Peter and Paul Cemetery, Marple Township, PA.

Tom Dougherty said Dennis was a great brother-in-law and he sincerely thought that Dennis would go all the way to a star or two (general) in his career. Tom and Dennis shared a number of good times together and Tom shall always remember him as his brother-in-law and a good guy. Dennis' death left a big hole in a lot of lives. Tom often wonders how things would have gone had Dennis lived. Dennis was a big influence on Tom's life and he still misses his friend every day.

Patricia described Dennis as bright, witty, and fun. He loved to travel and definitely enjoyed his duty assignments because of the opportunity to explore the new areas. He viewed them as "adventures." Dennis and Patricia would get a local map of the area, he would put his guitar in their car, an MG midget convertible, and off they'd go exploring his new duty station. She said Dennis was well respected by the troops he commanded and by his commanding officers. Dennis looked forward to a rewarding military career with the possibility of moving into the Foreign Service upon retiring from the military. Patricia states: "He was a devout Catholic, loved God and Country, and was proud to serve his country as an army officer." Patricia also said the effect of the loss of Dennis has been lifelong and the sorrow never seems to lessen.

This Chapter could only have been completed with Patricia's help and support. It has taken us over six months of constant contact. Thanks, Patricia. To Tom, thanks for all your help...your brother-in-law would be proud.

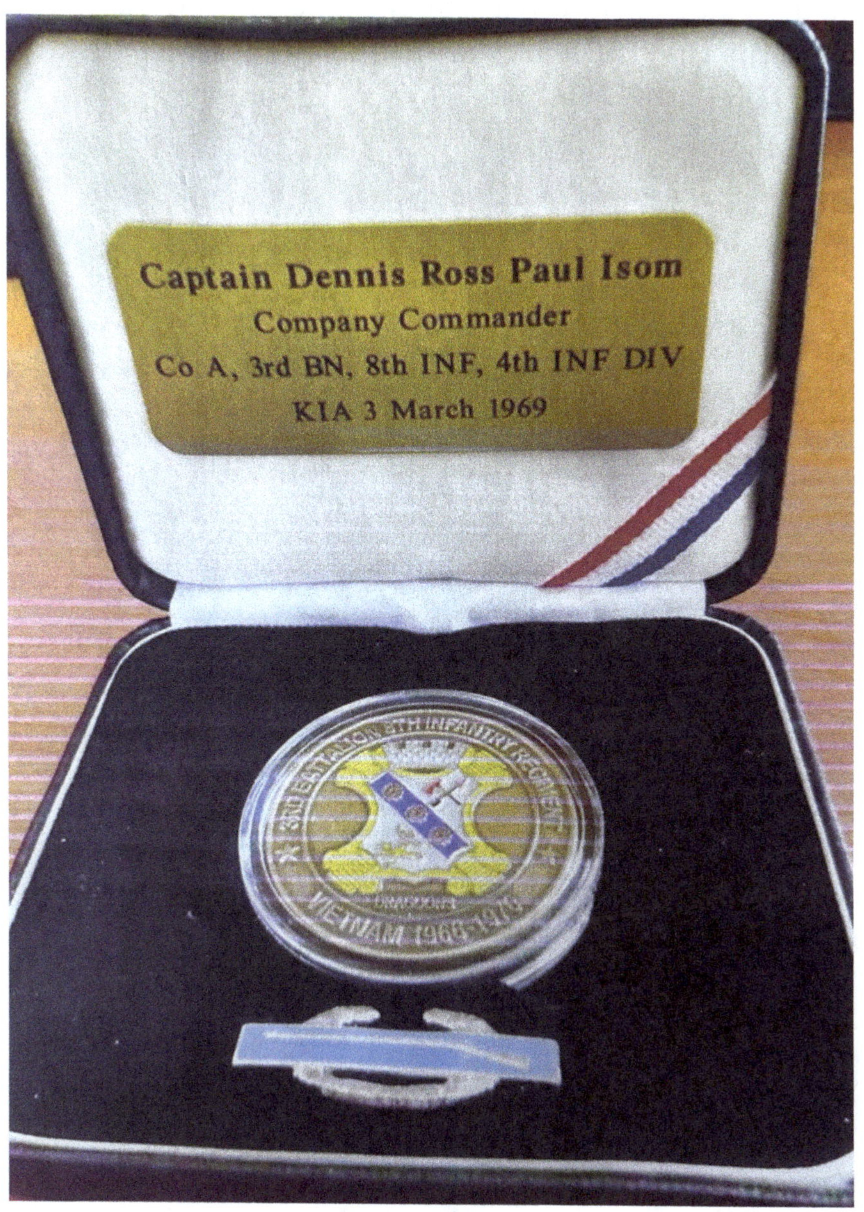

Sent to Dennis's widow, Patricia, after his death. The rest of the details, unfortunately, have faded with time.

Dennis was 24 years old, so young but proud of his service, his duty, the men he served with, and his country. It is an honor to call him my cadet Brother and fellow Vietnam Veteran... HOOAH!

This could be the last picture of Capt. Dennis Ross Paul Isom prior to the operation in Plei Trap Valley. Photo from "Ambush in Plei Trap Valley" by John F. Bauer.

Dennis Ross Paul Isom

Captain
A CO, 3RD BN, 8TH INFANTRY, 4TH INF DIV, USARV
Army of the United States
Drexel Hill, Pennsylvania
April 05, 1944 to March 03, 1969
DENNIS R ISOM is on the Wall at Panel W30, Line 25
See the full profile or name rubbing for Dennis Isom

10/22/22, 2:50 PM www.VirtualWall.org Profile

Dennis Ross Paul Isom

ON THE WALL: **Panel W30 Line 25**

This page Copyright© 1997-2018 www.VirtualWall.org Ltd.

PERSONAL DATA:

Home of Record:	Drexel Hill, PA
Date of birth:	04/05/1944

MILITARY DATA:

Service Branch:	Army of the United States
Grade at loss:	O3
Rank:	Captain
Promotion Note:	None
ID No:	OF108670
MOS:	1542: Infantry Unit Commander
Length Service:	02
Unit:	A CO, 3RD BN, 8TH INFANTRY, 4TH INF DIV, USARV

CASUALTY DATA:

Start Tour:	01/29/1969
Incident Date:	03/03/1969
Casualty Date:	03/03/1969
Status Date:	Not Applicable
Status Change:	Not Applicable
Age at Loss:	24
Location:	Kontum Province, South Vietnam
Remains:	Body recovered
Repatriated:	Not Applicable
Identified:	Not Applicable
Casualty Type:	Hostile, died outright
Casualty Reason:	Ground casualty
Casualty Detail:	Gun or small arms fire

URL: https:/www.VirtualWall.org/di/IsomDR01a.htm

Data accessed: 10/22/2022

THE VIRTUAL WALL ® www.VirtualWall.org

Print This Page Close This Page

Page template 10/09/2015

https://www.virtualwall.org/js/Profile.htm

CHAPTER 7: DANIEL FRANCIS MONAHAN

Dan was born in Chester, PA, and grew up in Glenolden. Daniel, the son of Francis and Edith Monahan, graduated from Interboro High School in 1958. Dan was in the PMC Class of 1962. From the feedback I received, Dan was one of the last "day hops" at PMC. He was active in the chess club, glee club, and a member of the Society for the Advancement of Management. His hobbies included chess and cars. He played intramural football for four years and was a member of the track team during his freshman year. In the 1962 yearbook (see above for his yearbook picture), he indicated that he planned to make the Army his career. He was voted as the outstanding cadet of the Senior class at the annual ROTC encampment. He graduated with a degree in Business Administration and was selected as Distinguished Military Student (DMS) (see next page) and was commissioned a Second Lieutenant in the Army in the Infantry.

Finest in 1961-62 Corps of Cadets

FRONT ROW (left to right)—Jack Christopher Kehoe III, Lawrence Bruce Krumanocker, Robert Ames Bellinger, Daniel True Madish, Robert John Adelmann, Bruce Martin Hanley, Joseph Michael Spadafina, William Nathaniel Simpson III, Stephen Prescott Rising, and Patrick Leno.
CENTER ROW — Joseph Salvador Berarducci, Anthony Augustine Prezioso, Daniel Francis Monahan, Louis Richard Palkovics, Lawrence Paul Gioielli, Robert Leslie Dainton, and William Ernest Muehsam.
BACK ROW — Frank William LiVolsi, Jr., Ross Anthony Cambareri, Jacques Bertrand Gerard, Joseph Albert DiEduardo, William Alfred Kester, Jr., Leonard Baryl Edelstein, Barry Lynn Ernst, Frank James Kovach, Jr.,Frank William Odiotti, and Edward Albert Steinmetz.

* * * * *

27 OUTSTANDING CADETS GET DISTINGUISHED RATINGS

Twenty-seven outstanding cadets at the College have been designated Distinguished Military Students for the 1961-62 school year. The honor places them in position to receive Regular U. S. Army Commissions upon graduation.

The requirements for this outstanding designation include high qualities of leadership, moral character and aptitude for military service. The selectees also had to be in the upper third of their Reserve Officers Training Corps (ROTC) classes, in the upper half of their classes academically, in addition to participation in campus activities.

All the designated cadets were closely observed at summer ROTC camp at Fort George Meade, Maryland.

The Distinguished Military Students are:

Robert John Adelmann, Robert Ames Bellinger, Joseph Salvador Berarducci, Ross Anthony Cambareri, Robert Leslie Dainton, Joseph Albert DiEduardo, Leonard Beryl Edelstein, Barry Lynn Ernst, Jacques Bertrand Gerard, Lawrence Paul Gioielli, Bruce Martin Hanley, Jack Christopher Kehoe III, William Alfred Kester, Jr., Frank James Kovach Jr.

Lawrence Bruce Krumanocker, Patrick Leno, Frank William LiVolsi, Jr., Daniel True Madish, Daniel Francis Monahan, William Ernest Muehsam, Frank William Odiotti, Louis Richard Palkovics, Anthony Augustine Prezioso, Stephen Prescott Rising, William Nathaniel Simpson III, Joseph Michael Spadafina, and Edward Albert Steinmetz.

DR. DASH JOINS FACULTY

President Clarence R. Moll announces the appointment of Dr. James Allen Dash, the noted choral director, as a replacement for Professor Donald Bermender of the English Department. Professor Bermender has been incapacitated by a protracted illness. Dr. Dash also directs the PMC Glee Club.

President Moll also disclosed the appointment of Mr. Fred Ulmer, former star wrestler at Drexel Institute of Technology, as a part-time assistant to PMC wrestling coach Harald Sveinbjornsson. Mr. Ulmer is an instructor and a football coach at Upper Darby High School.

24 ALUMNI BULLETIN • JANUARY 1962

Dan trained at Fort Lewis, Washington. He took paratrooper training at Fort Benning, Georgia and studied foreign languages at the Presidio in San Francisco. As a member of the Special Forces Green Beret, he spent 18 months in Panama before being sent to Vietnam as a member of the C Company, 2nd Battalion, 60th Infantry Regiment, 9th Infantry Division.

Capt. Daniel F. Monahan, Second from right, paratrooper training with fellow soldiers.

A Classmate of Dan's, Richard Handly, himself a retired military man of 23 years and a Major, recommended that I read a book titled *Mekong First Light* by Joseph W. Callaway Jr. Dan (in whose memory the book was written) and Calloway served together in Vietnam. I'm glad Richard made the recommendation. It was excellent! As Richard stated, the book tells about Dan's character and how he died a hero. He was loved and trusted by his men. Richard was also a day hop at PMC. As I'm writing this section, I have very little on Dan's personal life except that he was married to Elizabeth D. Cox and they had a daughter named Maureen, born eight days before Dan's death in Vietnam. In an article from *The Inquirer*, 4/18/67, Dan was in a chopper in Vietnam. He had been read a cablegram from his mother, Edith, He was a father. Why do I bring this up now, before we talk about Dan's action in Vietnam? The author, Joseph W. Callaway Jr, wrote a very emotional and moving letter to Maureen in 1984 in his book, talking to her about her dad and the type of man, friend, and soldier he was. l think Maureen would have been 17 years old when the book was published. The letter is one of the nicest things I have uncovered in researching these eight brave men. I've included it here because it discloses the quality of person Dan was.

The letter is from a man who worked for Dan as a platoon leader and trusted and respected Dan as a leader. Joe described Dan as..." a burly, bearlike man with an elfish twinkle in his eyes, who constantly tried to make me laugh. He had a wonderful Irish humor and always enjoyed creating a funny joke. Although he said I was too serious and worried too much, he always showed great confidence in my judgment. We would still be good friends today had he lived."

The date was April 14, 1967. Captain Dan Monahan was leading his Company in Long An Province, Republic of South Vietnam. The Company set up a defensive perimeter in a cracked, concrete-hard dry rice paddy. Captain Monahan's troops were exhausted having spent nine out of the last ten days in the field. At around 2200 hours (10:00 pm), Dan's troops came under fire from an enemy sniper. Captain Monahan and

Lt. Gray decided to call in artillery fire. Suddenly, a tremendous lightning flash and explosion filled the dark sky. In the morning, it was revealed that the blast was the result of three, banjo type Chinese claymore mines. They had been tied to a small tree and positioned only seven yards from the night perimeter. The Viet Cong had evidently been able to sneak up in the dark and place mines undetected. When remotely detonated, the mines released shrapnel, which was fatal to Captain Monahan and Lt. Gray. The medic, Spec 4 Peter Nero, raced to a wounded soldier while calling for the medic. There was nothing anyone could do for the soldier named McKee. He was dead. Nero went to Captain Monahan. His chest was torn apart and his lungs punctured. He was drowning in his own blood. Lt. Gray's head had been blown away. Captain Monahan was 27 years old.

Joseph W. Callaway Jr. said of Captain Monahan's leadership:

> During these soul searching days and between continual firefights, Captain Dan Monahan, who had replaced Bredleau after the February 26 Doi Mai Creek battle as the Charlie Company CO, became a refreshing guiding light. Dan had a good-spirited nature and a unique feel for people, and he enjoyed the leadership responsibility of motivating soldiers to stretch themselves to do better and achieve things they never thought possible. Dan brought new energy and courage to the company, and we all suddenly began to like one another instead of intensely competing. Dan's presence and demeanor stopped the junior officers, including me, from jockeying for power. He created a renewed spirit of teamwork.

Funeral services were held at the First Presbyterian Church in Glenolden, PA, on April 24, 1967. His internet was at Edgewood Memorial Park.

Letter to Dan Monahan's Daughter

June 24, 1984

Dear Maureen,

The past eighteen years, I am sure, seem long to you, but to me April 1967 was only yesterday. Your father and I were good friends. We knew each other only a few months but were bound inextricably together with the common purpose of doing our job and preserving life under the most dangerous and hostile conditions. We depended on each other. I was his point platoon leader, a young lieutenant. I was always the first guy in and the last guy out on every operation. We trusted each other's judgment.

We tried to bring some sanity to an environment of incredible violence. This life-and-death drama brought out the worst in many men—selfishness, hate, racism, fear, brutality, etc. I watched some men literally crumble before my eyes. Your dad provided a ray of hope in this harsh Vietnam world. He was concerned about human life. He was a good soldier, but more important he was a great man. He was concerned about others. He loved his fellow man. His bravery was commitment, and his courage was consistency. He was more a hero for his great compassion and character than for giving his life. His loss is our tragedy. He tried to build better people, and I shall always remember him.

In the days between your birth on April 6 and his death on April 14, he was very happy. Dan was very proud of his new daughter. He talked about you often. He always had that great Irish wit and subtle humor, and he was never better than during this period. I came to see you when you were a baby, but decided I could only bring sad memories to your mother and grandparents. For these many years, I have made no contact with your family but have always remembered. I knew

viii Letter to Dan Monahan's Daughter

you would be graduating from high school this year. The diamond pendant with the three connecting gold circles, which I have sent, not only is recognition of your achievement but is symbolic of your father's love for you, your mother, and your grandparents. I will always be a friend, and please stop by if you ever travel west.

Last fall, I went to Washington to visit the Vietnam Memorial. I found the names of many friends, including Daniel Francis Monahan. I was proud to have known your dad. He was a good friend.

Love,
Joe

the
PMC
alumnus

Volume 12 MAY 1967 Number 6

Published bi-monthly by PMC Alumni Association, PMC Colleges, Chester, Pa. 19013. Second class postage paid at Chester, Pa.

MEMBER, AMERICAN ALUMNI COUNCIL

THE PMC ALUMNI ASSOCIATION

BOARD OF MANAGERS

Oliver C. Armitage '49	*President*
William H. Turner '37	*1st V.P.*
William T. Burton, Jr. '31	*2nd V.P.*
Frederick F. Shahadi '49	*Secretary*
Frederick J. News, Jr. '50	*Treasurer*
Stewart C. Cresse '51	
M. Joseph Dwyer '53	
James B. Finnie '49	
J. Harold Hughes '59	
Sidney S. Mathues '51	
George B. Shaw, Jr. '27	
R. Brook Tomlinson '60	
Albert J. Westerman '29	

PAST PRESIDENTS' COUNCIL

J. A. G. Campbell, Jr. '20	(1931-35)
Carl A. Schaubel '30	(1941-43)
John R. Hanna '30	(1943-45)
Sherwyn L. Davis '26	(1949-51)
Weston C. Overholt '27	(1951-52)
C. Edgar Hires '34	(1952-53)
Edward C. Fay '36	(1953-55)
Stuart H. Raub '30	(1955-57)
Jesse W. Roberts '36	(1957-59)
Albert Frank '49	(1959-61)
Charles D. Hummer '27	(1961-63)
George E. Burke, Sr. '35	(1963-65)

C. Arthur Littman '60
Director of Alumni Relations

William J. Getty, Jr. *Editor*
Asst. Director of Alumni Relations

Howard F. Battin '22 *Staff Assistant*

Capt. Daniel F. Monahan '62 Killed By Land Mine in Action in Vietnam

Once again, the tragic toll of the war in Vietnam has struck home at PMC in all its terrifying intensity with news of the death of Capt. Daniel F. Monahan '62.

A career officer, and member of the elite Special Forces "Green Berets," he was killed by a land mine in Vietnam on April 14. Heightening the tragedy is the fact that his wife, Elizabeth, had given birth to a girl only eight days before.

At Pennsylvania Military College, Dan was a Business Administration major, a Distinguished Military student, and was voted the outstanding cadet of the senior class at ROTC encampment. He was a member of the Glee Club, Chess Club and S.A.M., played intramural football for four years, and was a member of the track team during his freshman year.

Immediately following graduation, in June 1962, he joined the Army and received a regular U. S. Army commission of 2/Lt.

He was transferred to Vietnam, shortly after he and his wife returned to his parents' home in Glenolden, Pa., from an 18-month tour of duty in Panama. He had been in Vietnam for four months.

Besides his wife, daughter Maureen, and his parents, Francis and Edith Monahan, he is survived by a sister, Mrs. Eleanor Cantarella, of Haddon Heights, N. J.

Funeral services on April 24 were attended by an honor guard from PMC.

CAPT. DANIEL F. MONAHAN '62

Engineering Seniors Show Project Results

Results of nine research projects by Pennsylvania Military College and Penn Morton College senior engineering students were presented at Kirkbride Hall on April 19.

Projects in general related to unsolved problems from current technology and involved small groups of students working in association with a faculty advisor.

Covering a wide variety of problems, the results included the development of a scale model lighter-than-air submarine simulator system; economic recovery of acetic acid from pulp mill waste cooking liquor; development of a polyurethane foam pore size meter; apt weather satellite receiving system; solids flow tunnel; gas turbine system; desorption characteristics of molecular sieves, model analysis of cable roofs and a concept for neighborhood development.

Six Cadets Awarded ROTC Scholarships

Six cadets have been selected as recipients of two-year Army ROTC scholarships.

The students, all sophomores, are: Robert N. Chinquina, Robert H. Heitman, Norman C. Helmold II, William W. Hoffman, George E. Mueller Jr., and James W. Pherson.

Providing full tuition, books and fees plus $50 per month during their junior and senior years, the scholarships are awarded on the basis of academic excellence, extracurricular activities, physical condition, College Entrance Examination Board tests, personal qualities and leadership potential.

Bill Muehsam Named To Admissions Post

Discharged from military service on March 3, William E. Muehsam '62, joined the PMC staff on March 13 as assistant director of Admissions.

Bill entered military service in Feb. '63 and from May '63 to Jan. '66 was stationed at Schofield Barracks, Hawaii.

In January 1966 he joined the 25th Division in Vietnam and saw action at Cu Chi and Pleiku. Wounded at Cu Chi by grenade fragments, he received the Purple Heart award.

He also was awarded the Bronze Star Medal in ceremonies at Tan Son Nhut for "outstanding meritorious service" in combat operations in Vietnam.

Ceremonies Honor Alumni Killed in Vietnam

At a ceremony in the Alumni Auditorium on Nov. 18 honoring four alumni killed in Vietnam, General James K. Woolnough, commanding general, U. S. Continental Army Command, unveils plaque provided by the Army in honor of Lt. John L. Geoghegan '63, killed in battle Nov. 15, 1965; Lt. William J. Stephenson '63, who fell in battle Feb. 23, 1966; and Capt. Daniel F. Monahan '62, killed April 14, 1967. Shown with Gen. Woolnough are, from left: Carol Stephenson, Betty Monaghan and Barbara Geoghegan.

In another undated picture of a ceremony, three of the wives of three of the PMC Alumni. Who were killed in Vietnam in this book, were honored by General James K. Woolnough. Please see below.

Mrs. Daniel F. Monahan holds Bronze Star awarded posthumously to Capt. Monahan '62 who lost his life in Vietnam on April 14. Col. Ford P. Fuller Jr., (right) Professor of Military Science made the presentation and Lt. Col. Henry G. Phillips, assistant to the president for Military Affairs, participated in the ceremony held in MacMorland Center.

In an article that appeared in the Delaware County Times on September 16, 1967, his widow, Elizabeth, received a Bronze Star that was awarded posthumously to her husband, Dan.

THE VIRTUAL WALL ® VIETNAM VETERANS MEMORIAL www.VIRTUALWALL.org

Find A Name ▼ The Virtual Wall® ▼ This Memorial Page ▼

Daniel Francis Monahan

Captain
C CO, 2ND BN, 60TH INFANTRY, 9TH INF DIV, USARV
Army of the United States
Norwood, Pennsylvania
February 15, 1940 to April 14, 1967
DANIEL F MONAHAN is on the Wall at Panel 18E, Line 26
See the full profile or name rubbing for Daniel Monahan

15 Feb 1999

Thinking of you on your Birthday

Charlie Oscar

A Note from The Virtual Wall

On 14 Apr 1967 Charlie Company, 2/60th Infantry, lost its Company Commander and four other men:

- **CPT Daniel F. Monahan, Norwood, PA**
- **PFC Joseph W. De Rosa, Deerfield, IL**
- **PFC Robert E. McKee, Eminence, KY**
- **PFC Robert Scherlag, New York, NY**
- **PFC Howard D. Vandenacre, Conrad, MT**

THE VIRTUAL WALL ® VIETNAM VETERANS MEMORIAL www.VIRTUALWALL.org

Contact Us © Copyright 1997-2019 www.VirtualWall.org, Ltd ®(TM) Last update 08/15/2019.

Probably the last picture taken of Cpt. Daniel F. Monahan in Vietnam before his death. The picture is from the book, Mekong First Light, by Joseph W. Callaway Jr.

Gone at 27 years old...too young. RIP my fellow PMC Cadet and Vietnam Veteran Brother. You are not forgotten!

8/24/22, 1:02 PM www.VirtualWall.org Profile

Daniel Francis Monahan

ON THE WALL: **Panel 18E Line 26**

This page Copyright© 1997-2018 www.VirtualWall.org Ltd.

PERSONAL DATA:

Home of Record:	Norwood, PA
Date of birth:	02/15/1940

MILITARY DATA:

Service Branch:	Army of the United States
Grade at loss:	O3
Rank:	Captain
Promotion Note:	None
ID No:	O95633
MOS:	1542: Infantry Unit Commander
Length Service:	04
Unit:	C CO, 2ND BN, 60TH INFANTRY, 9TH INF DIV, USARV

CASUALTY DATA:

Start Tour:	10/12/1966
Incident Date:	04/14/1967
Casualty Date:	04/14/1967
Status Date:	Not Applicable
Status Change:	Not Applicable
Age at Loss:	27
Location:	Long An Province, South Vietnam
Remains:	Body recovered
Repatriated:	Not Applicable
Identified:	Not Applicable
Casualty Type:	Hostile, died outright
Casualty Reason:	Ground casualty
Casualty Detail:	Multiple fragmentation wounds
URL:	https://VirtualWall.org/dm/MonahanDF01a.htm
Data accessed:	8/24/2022

THE VIRTUAL WALL ® www.VirtualWall.org

Print This Page Close This Page

Page template 10/09/2015

https://virtualwall.org/js/Profile.htm

CHAPTER 8: WILLIAM (BUD) JAMES STEPHENSON

William James "Bud" Stephenson grew up on Crescent Avenue in Spotswood, NJ, despite what the Vietnam Virtual Wall says. He went to Pennsylvania Military College in the Class of '63 where he majored in Accounting. He played the trumpet and was a member of the band, the Dance Band (his future wife, Carol, sang with them), and the Glee Club. He enjoyed competing in football, track, and wrestling. Bud is well remembered for his vitality, his industry, and his honesty. Above is his Senior picture from the Class Yearbook.

Bud was born in the Bronx, NY. His Dad was a naval officer and the family moved around a lot. In high school, he played in the marching band, worked in theater productions, ran track. Carol, the former Carol Apone, told me that when he lived in New Jersey, Bud was proudest of attending Boys' State via the local American Legion Post and being an Eagle Scout. Bud met Carol at the Teen Club at the American Legion Post in Spotswood, NJ and they dated for three years. While at PMC (according to Ken Whilden, a classmate of Bud's), Bud wanted to propose to Carol but could not afford a ring. So Bud improvised a way to earn the money to buy the ring. (I'll let it go at that.) Ken said Bud was a great guy, full of fun, but could also be serious. Bud was in the band (Headquarters Company) and Ken was Company Commander of D Company. Bud was a good friend and always made time for Ken. Bud and Carol were married on June 22, 1963, two weeks after Bud graduated from Pennsylvania Military College.

Upon graduation, Bud was commissioned a 2nd Lieutenant and went to Fort Benning, GA, for infantry officer basic training. He then reported to Fort Rucker, Alabama, for fixed wing flight training. On May 30, 1964, Carol gave birth to identical twins but sadly, one was stillborn. The surviving twin was named William. When Bud's fixed wing training was completed, he was assigned to Fort Campbell, Kentucky, as the personal pilot for Colonel Bill Talon. Bud was ordered to switch to rotary (helicopter) training and was reassigned to Mineral Wells, Texas. Carol and their son joined him in Texas. Bud was going to make the military his career and Carol had no objection. Bud always wanted to fly.

On January 2, 1966, with his son only 20 months old and Carol expecting their second child, Bud left for Vietnam. Carol's Father took Bud to the airport to go to San Francisco, CA, and then onto Vietnam. Bud asked his father-in law to make him a promise...to take care of his family if he didn't come back from Vietnam. It was not until after Bud's death that Carol found out about Bud's premonition. When Bud arrived in Vietnam, he was assigned to A Troop, 1st Squadron, 9th Cavalry, 1st Cavalry Division, as a Rotary Wing Aviation Unit Commander, in An-Khe, South Vietnam. In Bud's unit was Rex Dula, a CWO (Chief Warrant Officer) and Squadron instructor pilot in charge of transitioning Bud into the OH-13S scout helicopter or the "bubble gum machine." They didn't spend a lot of time at the base camp.

Bud and Carol's wedding day, June 22, 1963, Immaculate Conception Church in Spotswood, NJ.

The PMC Cadets in the Saber Arch. On the right are Harry Mazur and Warren Kaiser and on the left Albert Nicola and Warren (Buzz) Miller.

This is Bud with his son Brett in Fort Campbell, KY just prior to Bud receiving his orders for Vietnam.

Bell OH-13 Sioux
Posted by Stephenson, William James, 1LT

Tail # 63-09210

The description of the subsequent events is absolutely amazing to me. I spent four years at a military high school, four years at a military college, and almost three years in the US Army in Germany and Vietnam, and never heard of such heroism "firsthand" in my life. I hope I can do their unbelievable bravery the justice it deserves. I personally spoke to Rex Dula and his observer/gunner, Bobby Pridmore, the machine gunner on Rex's chopper, but his wife, Judy, said he was physically unable to talk on the phone.

She told tell me that Bobby was the most decorated Veteran in Block County, TN, where they live. What I'm about to relate to the reader is true as told to me in person and as researched in documents provided to me by Rex Dula or Carol from the actual participants in the shooting down of Lt. Bud Stephenson.

The day was February 19, 1966, in an area of South Vietnam known as Bong Son. Lt. Bud Stephenson, a scout pilot, and his observer, PFC Kenneth Wayne Lanter, were on a reconnaissance mission in their OH-13S helicopter looking for VC (Viet Cong) and NVA (North Vietnam Army). The weather was bad with dense fog and low ceilings. Due to the weather, the mission was delayed, so they sat around and shot the breeze. Bud talked about his family and how proud he was of his son and the baby on the way. The weather broke and they decided to launch the mission. Bud was scout lead with his observer. CWO Rex Dula flying a Huey and his observer Bobby Pridmore were flying about 100 yards behind. As Dula crossed the ridgeline, his chopper started to take on intense automatic weapons fire through the floor and radios in the front instrument panel. Bud heard part of Dula's transmission and turned to draw fire from Dula. Dula tried to tell Bud, "13 roll out, it's too hot." Bud also came under intense automatic weapons fire. Here are Dula's own words.

> When he was directly facing the automatic weapons is probably when Kenny was hit in the head and as Bud turned right is when Bud was most likely hit, causing him to roll the aircraft inverted. The helicopter impacted inverted and one of the fuel cells tore loose and flew about 50 ft. away from the impact site. At first, I thought one of them had been thrown clear. No such luck.

Bud had crashed in a dry rice paddy with NVA in the area and along the river bank. Dula made two rocket runs and Pridmore fired his M60 to suppress the firing around the downed chopper. Rex looked down at the wreckage and saw movement. As he found out later, Kenny was hit in the head and died instantly from his wounds. Bud was hit with eleven rounds but survived the crash.

As Rex hovered near the crash site, the NVA were firing from positions 50 yards on one side and about 75 yards on the other side of his aircraft. Bobby Pridmore was firing his M6O. Rex and Bobby were out of radio contact. No one knew where they were. Bobby told Rex to "put me down beside them and go for help." The next thing Rex saw was Bobby jumping out of the chopper with his M6O in hand and an ammo box between his legs. When he landed in the wreckage, he shielded Bud and Kenny with his own body. As Rex prepared to leave, he circled and made a few rocket runs on the NVA until his rockets were expended. On his last pass, a round hit the Plexiglas beside his left cheek. He said it felt like slap in the face; he knew he had to go. Rex said, "One of the hardest things I ever had to do was to fly away leaving them there. I truly believed I would never see them alive again."

When Dula arrived at Bong Son, he could smell the gas coming out of the bullet holes in the fuel tank and pouring over his hot engine. He said it should have caught on fire. He reported to the Operations Officer who told Rex he had already assigned a craft and crew to rescue the downed crew. Rex went over to the chopper, pulled the gunner off the craft, and took his seat behind the M60. On the way to rescue Bud and Kenny, the chopper Dula was in was shot down into a river with the NVA firing all around them. A chopper from the blue platoon picked them up from the river. Upon returning to Bong Son, another chopper was preparing to leave. Dula took this M60 gunner's place on a Huey B model.

When they arrived at the crash site, Bobby Pridmore was able to keep the NVA from overrunning the crash site. Again, let me quote Rex Dula on what he observed.

> The last time I saw him, [Bobby] was lying beside Bud shielding his body with his own. He told me that when he saw us coming he was down to the last three rounds for the M60 and one round in his 38 pistol. The last round was for himself if he was overrun. Lord, where do we get

> such brave young men. You, Lord, said, "Greater love has no man than to lay down his life for his fellow man." This was 19-year-old Bobby Pridmore.

The entire operation took about one hour. I can't even imagine. Young Bobby Pridmore stayed with Bud and Kenny, protecting them from the NVA with his M6O and his 38. Rex and Bobby wanted to protect them from the NVA because whether they were dead or alive, an NVA soldier was paid a bounty for capturing a member or bringing in a dead body from a chopper crew. Rex said: "Warrant Officers Baron and Talley as well as their crews were mutilated after being shot down." Horrible to even think that happened.

According to Tom Tiede, author of an article entitled "A Soldier's Death in Viet Nam," it took ten men to move the scrap enough so that those inside could be pulled free. Bud was rushed to a hospital. He was wounded 11 times over his body and once in the neck. Tom also stated: "They operated and they prayed and they did all they could...but it was too late. The wounds, the crash, and the crush of the wreckage won out." Bud died on 2/23/66; four days after he crashed. He was 24 years old.

I asked Rex Dula to tell me about Bud Stephenson, the pilot and the man. Rex said Bud was always smiling, laid back, a helluva good scout pilot, a great team player, and a very good leader who led by example. This comes from a man who should know: 27 and a half years in the service and retired as a CW4.

After I talked to Rex and read his documentation on this event, I was very impressed by the bravery, heroism, devotion, and camaraderie of the men in this action. I can't even imagine what was going through Bud's mind as he lay in his chopper's wreckage, helpless, severely wounded, next to his young, dead comrade while Bobby Pridmore protected them from becoming victims of NVA brutality. For his actions, Bobby Pridmore was awarded the Silver Star for bravery. The paperwork was submitted for him to receive the Medal of Honor. At the time of the writing of this book, it was stuck in red tape and no decision had been made yet.

One of Bud Stephenson's classmates from the Class of '63 at Pennsylvania Military College was John R. Stoeffler. John met Bobby Pridmore at an event at PMC and was so inspired by their discussions in regards to Bud being shot down that he wrote a poem included on the next page. Thanks John, excellent job!

A BAD DAY AT BONG SON (RVN)

(A True Story)

By John R. Stoeffler

'Twas the 19th of February one nine sixty-six
Soon "A" Troop of the 9th Cav would be in the thick.
Another day of fighting in the Vietnam War
Bobby Pridmore manned a 60 at his chopper's door.

Fog covered the valley where no wind did blow
It looked like a whiteout at home when it snows.
At nine the fog lifted they were headed southwest
All had a feeling they'd soon face a daunting test.

Flying just above the treetops bullets hit the chopper's frame
Radios were blasted 'twas now a deadly game.
Pridmore lowered his 60 returning fire from below
He held the trigger down, tracers making quite a show.

Nearby, "Buddy" Stephenson clearly saw their plight
Firing 60s on his chopper's skids he swept from left to right.
NVA returned fire, Pridmore saw "Buddy" hit
He crashed in a rice paddy with a dike surrounding it.

Chief Dula flew the chopper that was Pridmore's that day
To the south of where "Buddy" crashed NVA held sway.
51 Cal. Machine guns opened up on the crash site
Dula fired back with rockets, NVA ducked out of sight.

They were taking hits as Dula set his chopper down
Pridmore loosed his seat belt and dropped to the ground.
"I'll stay with Stephenson" he yelled, "get help on the way!"
Three NVA charged toward him it was not their lucky day.

Pridmore took them out, and by Buddy's side he lay
Shielding him from harm though his life might end that day.
Bobby scavenged ammo from the chopper that went down
Holding off the NVA who were scattered all around.

Dula signaled Pridmore, he waved to come to him
NVA were closing fast, situation looking grim
Pridmore waved him off, he would stay by Buddy's side
For an hour he held the bad guys off, now it was do or die

"A" Troop sent a gun ship and a platoon of Infantry
To rescue Bobby and Buddy from the closing enemy.
Three rounds left for his 60 and two for his 38
It was time to saddle up before it was too late.

All wounded were picked up and flown to their home base,
Time was of the essence, there was no time to waste.
Buddy was gravely wounded, he was barely alive.
Medical help was waiting for the wounded to arrive.

But Buddy finally passed away, sent home to his final rest.
A salute was fired, taps were played, friends and family grieved.
Buddy was now laid to rest, in heaven he was received.

Decades have passed since that day when on the battlefield they met
It was a day that Pridmore said he'll never 'ere forget.
And I know that one day when war will be no more
Bobby and Buddy will meet again in the mansions of the Lord.

END

For his heroic, selfless action on February 19, 1966 while attempting to rescue First Lieutenant William J. "Buddy" Stephenson, 19-year-old PFC Bobby R. Pridmore was awarded the Silver Star.

Copyright 2018
John R.Stoeffler
5108 Brittany Drive #302
St. Petersburg, FL 33715

Another Classmate of Bud's, Ken Whilden, then a Lieutenant, along with an Army Chaplain, informed Carol of Bud's death. Ken Whilden was assigned as the escort officer to bring Bud back to New Jersey. Ken accompanied the body home from Oakland, CA. When we spoke about this in September 2022, Ken almost began crying recalling this memory. It has been over 56 years since Bud's death and it still has an impact on him. Ken is a retired Colonel with 34 years of service in the US Army as an Infantry and Armor officer. Bud's viewing was on Sunday, March 6, 1966, with burial in Beverly National Cemetery, NJ, on Monday, March 7th. Attending the services from Pennsylvania Military College were a Cadet Honor Guard, pallbearers, and two Cadet Buglers. Carol said two Cadets, one on each side of Bud's casket, stood vigil all night. It was impressive. She also said that Major General Biddle attended the service in his full dress uniform. The funeral home marked Carol's bill "Paid in Full" as a thank you for Bud's sacrifice.

Another Heart To Cheer Fallen Viet Nam Pilot

Kelly Ann Stephenson will never see her father but she'll know he was a man to make her proud. Kelly Ann was born at 8 a.m. yesterday at St. Peter's Hospital to Mrs. Carol Apone Stephenson, widow of First Lt. William J. (Buddy) Stephenson, helicopter pilot shot down in Viet Nam on Feb. 19.

Mrs. Stephenson was to be an honored guest at Memorial Day ceremonies Monday in Highland Park, but she'll be at St. Peter's Hospital during the ceremonies, instead.

Mrs. Stephenson's mother, Mrs. Harry Apone, said, "Everyone thought Carol would have a boy, but my son-in-law was the only one who predicted correctly that a girl would be born." The couple's first child, William James, will be two years old Monday, Memorial Day.

Formerly a resident of 352 Crowells Road, Highland Park, Mrs. Stephenson and her children now live at 447 Wheeler Place, Somerset, with her parents, Mr. and Mrs. Harry Apone.

Stephenson was on a combat mission near Bong Son, South Veit Nam, when his helicopter was hit by enemy ground fire Feb. 19. He died four days later on Ash Wednesday. The Army notified his widow he had been posthumously awarded the Purple Heart,

Kelly was born on 5/28/66

I've enclosed two letters to Carol on her loss. One was from Major General William S. Biddle, then Advisor for Military Affairs at PMC and later the Commandant, and another from C. Arthur Littman, '60, Director of Alumni Relations.

26 February 1966

Mrs. William J. Stephenson
352 Crowell Avenue
Highland Park, N. J.

Dear Mrs. Stephenson:

All of us at P. M. C. who knew your husband are deeply grieved to learn of his death in Vietnam. It is a great tragedy and we send our profound sympathy.

I remember Bill so well, to include his really outstanding military bearing. I am certain that he gave a fine account of himself over there and was a great credit to his country, his unit, his College and of course his family.

We genuinely share your grief, and we stand ready to help you in any way we can.

Sincerely,

WILLIAM S. BIDDLE
Major General, U. S. A. (Ret.)
Advisor for Military Affairs

February 26, 1966

Mrs. Carol Stephenson
352 Crowells Road
Highland Park, New Jersey 08901

Dear Mrs. Stephenson:

On behalf of the entire alumni body of Pennsylvania Military College, may I express our sincere sympathy to you on the untimely death of your husband Bill. It was my personal pleasure to know Buddy, when he was at PMC, and I feel this loss very deeply.

I am sure that many people will offer many words of condolence and sympathy to you at this trying time in your life. However, we of the Alumni Association want you to know that we share in your loss and stand ready to offer our services to you at any time. A young man who has made the supreme sacrifice in the defense of the freedom which our country so vividly is willing to defend, makes us very proud to have had him a member of our instution. We have been advised that 1/Lt. Kenneth Whilden is handling the arrangements for your husband, and that he will be keeping us informed.

As you probably know, Carol, at a time like this words can never express all that people really feel, and therefore I will not try and elaborate on our feelings, but just hope that you will realize that we are thinking of you and extremely sorry to learn the sad news.

Very sincerely,

C. Arthur Littman, '60
Director of Alumni Relations

CAL/epe

Ceremonies Honor Alumni Killed in Vietnam

At a ceremony in the Alumni Auditorium on Nov. 18 honoring four alumni killed in Vietnam, General James K. Woolnough, commanding general, U. S. Continental Army Command, unveils plaque provided by the Army in honor of Lt. John L. Geoghegan '63, killed in battle Nov. 15, 1965; Lt. William J. Stephenson '63, who fell in battle Feb. 23, 1966; and Capt. Daniel F. Monahan '62, killed April 14, 1967. Shown with Gen. Woolnough are, from left: Carol Stephenson, Betty Monaghan and Barbara Geoghegan.

THE VIRTUAL WALL ® VIETNAM VETERANS MEMORIAL www.VIRTUALWALL.org

Find A Name ▼ The Virtual Wall® ▼ This Memorial Page ▼

William James Stephenson

First Lieutenant

A TRP, 1ST SQDN, 9TH CAVALRY, 1ST CAV DIV, USARV

Army of the United States

Bound Brook, New Jersey

June 06, 1941 to February 23, 1966

(Incident Date February 19, 1966)

WILLIAM J STEPHENSON is on the Wall at Panel 5E, Line 69

See the full profile or name rubbing for William Stephenson

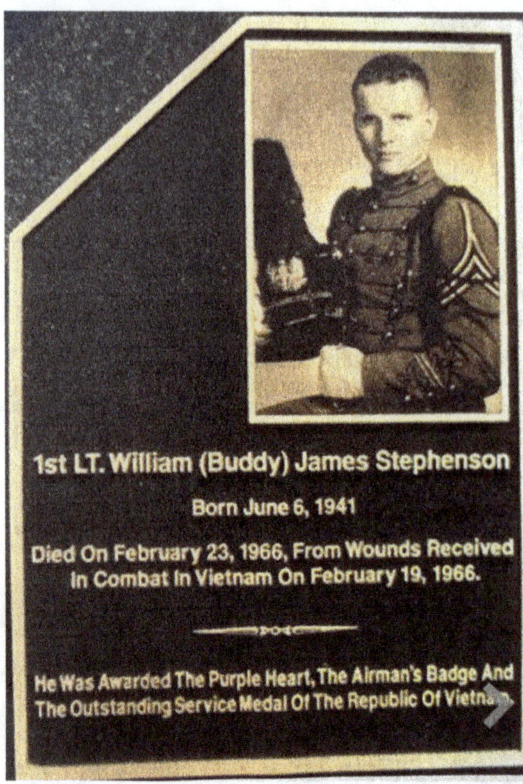

1st LT. William (Buddy) James Stephenson
Born June 6, 1941
Died On February 23, 1966, From Wounds Received
In Combat In Vietnam On February 19, 1966.
He Was Awarded The Purple Heart, The Airman's Badge And
The Outstanding Service Medal Of The Republic Of Vietnam

23 Sep 2005

I am the son of William James Stephenson.

I too was born with his name but as I was a twin and my twin brother died (we were to be named Brett and Bart - Maverick-style), although I was legally William, I was called Brett. I now live in Enniskerry, County Wicklow, Ireland and I think about my dad every day. I was not even 2 when he was killed. I know he is watching over me and my sister and my family. I still maintain his sword from the Pennsylvania Military Academy and have all of his medals and letters as well as some of his uniforms but I would rather have had him alive.

From his son,
Brett James Stephenson
Ireland
sirbong@yahoo.com

28 Oct 2005

Bud and I were married on June 22, 1963, two weeks after he graduated from Pennsylvania Military College in Chester, Pennsylvania. We had identical twin sons one year later (May 30, 1966). Unfortunately, one son was stillborn. On January 2, 1966 when our son was 20 months old, Bud left for Vietnam. While he originally trained as a fixed-wing pilot, he transitioned to helicopters as the need arose. I was pregnant with our second child. His helicopter was shot down on February 19, 1966 and he died of his injuries four days later on February 23, 1966. Our daughter, Kelly, was born 3 months later on May 18, 1966. He was an Eagle Scout, a fine cadet, an exemplary soldier and a man of honor. He made his family and his country proud. He will remain in our hearts as long as we live.

From his wife,
Carol Stephenson DeBunda
cad8@psu.edu

A Note from The Virtual Wall

A Troop, 1st Sqdn, 9th Cavalry, lost an OH-13S observation helicopter (tail number 63-09210) on 19 Feb 1966, shot down while on a reconnaissance mission. Two men died as a result of the incident:

- 1LT William James Stephenson, pilot, died on 23 Feb 1966 of wounds received
- PFC Kenneth Wayne Lanter, observer, died in the crash

THE VIRTUAL WALL ® VIETNAM VETERANS MEMORIAL www.VIRTUALWALL.org

Contact Us © Copyright 1997-2019 www.VirtualWall.org, Ltd ®(TM) Last update 08/15/2019.

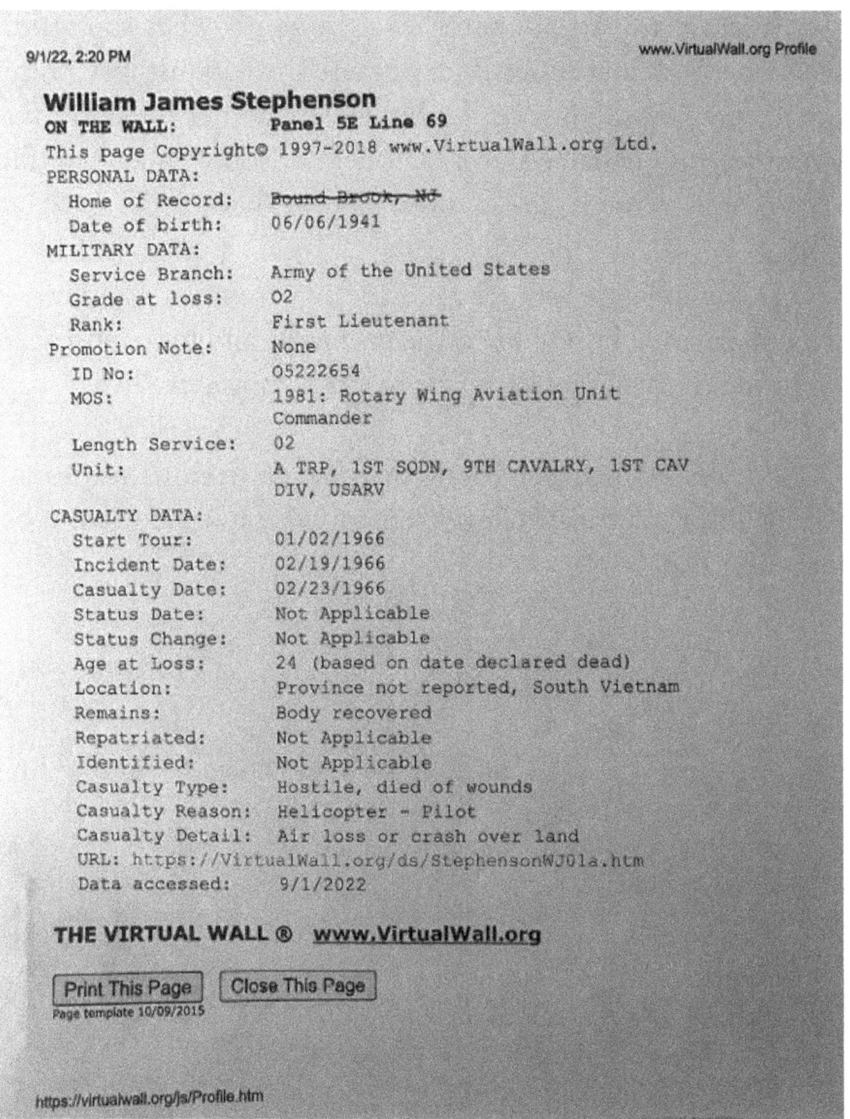

9/1/22, 2:20 PM www.VirtualWall.org Profile

William James Stephenson

ON THE WALL: **Panel 5E Line 69**

This page Copyright© 1997-2018 www.VirtualWall.org Ltd.

PERSONAL DATA:

Home of Record:	~~Bound Brook, NJ~~
Date of birth:	06/06/1941

MILITARY DATA:

Service Branch:	Army of the United States
Grade at loss:	O2
Rank:	First Lieutenant
Promotion Note:	None
ID No:	O5222654
MOS:	1981: Rotary Wing Aviation Unit Commander
Length Service:	02
Unit:	A TRP, 1ST SQDN, 9TH CAVALRY, 1ST CAV DIV, USARV

CASUALTY DATA:

Start Tour:	01/02/1966
Incident Date:	02/19/1966
Casualty Date:	02/23/1966
Status Date:	Not Applicable
Status Change:	Not Applicable
Age at Loss:	24 (based on date declared dead)
Location:	Province not reported, South Vietnam
Remains:	Body recovered
Repatriated:	Not Applicable
Identified:	Not Applicable
Casualty Type:	Hostile, died of wounds
Casualty Reason:	Helicopter - Pilot
Casualty Detail:	Air loss or crash over land

URL: https://VirtualWall.org/ds/StephensonWJ01a.htm

Data accessed: 9/1/2022

THE VIRTUAL WALL ® www.VirtualWall.org

Print This Page Close This Page

Page template 10/09/2015

https://virtualwall.org/js/Profile.htm

I want to express my deep appreciation to Carol, Bud's widow, and Rex Dula for their support through pictures, numerous emails, documents, and one-on-one conversations that at times were difficult and emotional. Without them, this tribute to Bud's bravery and heroism would not be complete. Thank you both!

I asked Carol to put into her own words what she wants the reader to know about Bud. Because she had just lost a dear friend, she said she just couldn't do it. I read her the entry she wrote on the Virtual Wall on October 28, 2005, and asked if it was all right to use it. She said yes. Here are her words.

> He was an Eagle Scout, a fine cadet, an exemplary soldier and a man of honor. He made his family and his country proud. He will remain in our hearts as long as we live.

Bud was 24, another young man, taken from us too soon. RIP Fellow Cadet and Fellow Vietnam Veteran...you will not be forgotten!

CHAPTER 9:
DAVID RALPH WILSON

Here is Dave's senior picture from the Class of 1966 PMC Yearbook.

Dave was brought up in Oreland, PA, by his parents, Mr. and Mrs. David M. Wilson, who lived at 311 Lorraine Avenue in Oreland with his sister Ellen. Dave attended and graduated from Springfield Senior High School in Montgomery County prior to attending Pennsylvania Military College in the Class of 1966. While at PMC, Dave majored in Economics and was active in the Circle K Club, SAM (Society for the Advancement of Management), the Young Republicans, and enjoyed playing intramurals. I remember Dave as a Brother in Tau Kappa Epsilon Fraternity. A good friend of Dave's at PMC was Steve Tochterman. In Steve's words, Dave was one of his best buddies at PMC. Steve said Dave was a first class person, a great guy, kind, and diligent. Dave was very proud that he had achieved the highest level in scouting, Eagle. Steve used to go to TKE parties with Dave and considered himself a "social" TKE. Dave's sister Ellen, dated and eventually married a PMC Cadet named Joe Holler, Class of '64.

At graduation from PMC in 1966, Dave was commissioned as a 2nd Lieutenant in the US Army in the Transportation Corps, the same branch as mine. There is little or no information available on Dave's military service. I would assume Dave attended the Transportation Officers Basic Course (TOBC) at Fort Eustis, VA, sometime in middle-to-late 1966. This is a guess based on my experience as a Transportation Officer myself. With that in mind, unless I receive more information on his military service, let's proceed to Dave's tour in Vietnam.

Dave arrived in Vietnam on August 14, 1967, and was assigned to the 64th Transportation Company, 124th Transportation Battalion, 8th Transportation Group, Army Support Command, Qui Nhon in Binh Dinh Province. On January 31, 1968, 1st LT Wilson was in charge of a supply convoy of five-ton tractor trailers returning to An Khe from Pleiku. At the foot of Mang Yang Pass, the convoy was ambushed by a superior enemy force using mortar and small arms fire. Many of the vehicles in the convoy stopped and were in the middle of the intense enemy fire. When the attack began, 1st LT Wilson's command vehicle was just forward of the kill zone. Even though he was out of danger, Dave immediately returned to the kill zone with utter disregard for his own safety and led his men to safety. While directing the convoy out of harm's way, his jeep sustained a direct hit from a mortar round. He died of multiple fragmentation wounds. 1st LT David Ralph Wilson was 23 years old.

Funeral services were held on February 20, 1968, at Christ Lutheran Church in Oreland, PA. He was survived by his parents, Mr. and Mrs. David M. Wilson, Jr., and a sister, Ellen. Six PMC Cadets served as pallbearers and the Commandant's Staff and others from PMC attended the service. One of those pallbearers, Jim "Spike" Pierson, remembers the funeral director advising the group that the casket would be "light" because the jeep had taken a direct mortar hit. It was a sobering' moment. Dave was buried at the Whitemarsh Memorial Park, Ambler, Montgomery County, PA.

the
PMC
alumnus

Volume 13 MARCH 1968 Number 5

Published bi-monthly by PMC Alumni Association, PMC Colleges, Chester, Pa. 19013. Second class postage paid at Chester, Pa.

MEMBER, AMERICAN ALUMNI COUNCIL

John R. McCullough '39, *Director of Alumni Relations*

William J. Getty, Jr., *Editor*, *Asst. Director of Alumni Relations*

THE PMC ALUMNI ASSOCIATION

BOARD OF MANAGERS

William H. Turner '37 — *President*
William T. Burton Jr. '31 — *1st V.P.*
Sidney S. Mathues '51 — *2nd V.P.*
Frederick F. Shahadi '49 — *Secretary*
Frederick J. News, Jr. '50 — *Treasurer*
Howard F. Battin, Jr. '57
John A. Bremble, Jr. '49
Edward H. Coleman '49
M. Joseph Dwyer '53
J. Harold Hughes, Jr. '59
Robert H. Peoples '43
William P. Petit de Mange '50
George B. Shaw, Jr. '27
R. Brook Tomlinson '60
S. Allen Wolf '54

PAST PRESIDENTS' COUNCIL

Oliver C. Armitage '49 (1965-67)
George E. Burke, Sr. '35 (1963-65)
Charles D. Hummer '27 (1961-63)
Albert Frank '49 (1959-61)
Jesse W. Roberts '36 (1957-59)
Stuart H. Raub '30 (1955-57)
Edward C. Fay '38 (1953-55)
C. Edgar Hires '34 (1952-53)
Weston C. Overholt '27 (1951-52)
Sherwyn L. Davis '26 (1949-51)
John R. Hanna '30 (1943-45)
Carl A. Schaubel '30 (1941-43)
J. A. G. Campbell, Jr. '20 (1931-35)

Board of Managers meets in Alumni Auditorium at 7:30 p.m., May 15, 1968.

Lieut. David R. Wilson '66 Killed By Mortar Fire in Central Vietnam

1/Lt. David R. Wilson '66 lost his life in the Vietcong offensive in Central Vietnam on Jan. 31. He died as the result of multiple fragmentation wounds received when a vehicle in which he was riding came under heavy mortar attack between An Khe and Pleiku.

Funeral services were held on Feb. 20 in Christ Lutheran Church, Oreland, Pa.

Members of the colleges' administration, faculty and staff, and the Commandant's staff, attended the services. Six Cadets who served as pall bearers were: Charles Cantley, Thomas Dougherty, James Mady, John Parry, John Pierson and William Potts.

Cadets William Feyk and Stuart Perlmutter were buglers.

Lieut. Wilson is survived by his parents, Mr. and Mrs. David M. Wilson, Jr., 311 Lorraine Avenue, Oreland, and a sister who is the wife of Joseph C. Holler '64.

In lieu of flowers at the funeral, his parents requested that donations be sent to Christ Lutheran Church or Pennsylvania Military College.

As a student, Lieut. Wilson was Cadet Aide to Commandant Menard. A member of Tau Kappa Epsilon, he was treasurer of the Theta Lambda Chapter in his junior and senior years. He also was a member of the Circle K Club and the Society for Advancement of Management.

Lieut. Wilson is the fifth alumnus to lose his life in the Vietnam conflict. Others are: Lt. (j.g.) Joseph R. Mossman '61, Lt. John L. Geoghegan '63, Lt. William J. Stephenson '63 and Capt. Daniel F. Monahan '62.

WORKSHOPS EXAMINING URBAN AREA PROBLEMS

A 14-week seminar-workshop series on urban problems is being sponsored by the colleges' Joint Center for Urban Affairs in MacMorland Center.

Held on consecutive Wednesdays, the program, which started on Feb. 7, is a non-credit offering particularly for health and welfare professionals. It is designed to bring the perspectives of a variety of disciplines to bear on urban problems.

Directed by Prof. Leonard Mann, the Joint Center is primarily concerned with assisting public officials, leaders of private organizations, and interested citizens and students involved with urban affairs.

Penn Morton Students Host Conference on College Life

Penn Morton College played host to the second Annual Conference on College Life and Affairs, Feb. 9 and 10.

In the two-day conference, discussions ranged from academic freedom, curriculum planning and policy making to classroom learning and extra-curricular activities.

Student speakers included Bart Cranston, president of Penn Morton's student government association; William Steel, a member of the student Senate; and William Knaus, co-editor of the Yearbook and chairman of the faculty evaluation committee.

J. WETHERILL SUCCUMBS IN FT. LAUDERDALE, FLA.

John L. Wetherill '05 died in Fort Lauderdale, Fla., on February 24. He was 81.

Funeral services were held in Chester on February 28.

Surviving are his wife, Naomi, and a sister, Mrs. Florence Wetherill Wilson.

Following his graduation from PMC in 1905 with a civil engineer's degree, he received the master's degree from Cornell University in 1907.

His former home at 14th and Potter Streets in Chester is now the Penn Morton co-ed dormitory.

3

On May 3, 1968, in ceremonies at Pennsylvania Military College, Dave's parents, Mr. and Mrs. David M. Wilson, accepted the Silver Star, presented posthumously to their son, 1st LT David Wilson, by Colonel Ford Fuller, Commandant of the PMC Cadet Corps. The Silver Star is the nation's third highest award for heroism. The Silver Star citation for 1st LT Wilson reads as follows:

The Silver Star

David R. Wilson

First Lieutenant
United States Army
64th Transportation Company
Place and Date: 31 January 1968
Twenty Miles West of An Khe, Republic of Vietnam

For gallantry in action while engaged in military operations against an armed hostile force in the Republic of Vietnam. First Lieutenant David R. Wilson, Transportation Corps, United States Army, who distinguished himself on 31 January 1968 while serving as Commander of a supply convoy in the Republic of Vietnam. Approximately twenty miles west of An Khe, Republic of Vietnam, First-Lieutenant Wilson's convoy was subjected to fire by an enemy force. Although he was safely out of the danger zone, he unhesitatingly returned to the scene of the action to lead his men to safety. Many of the vehicles had halted in the kill zone and were subject to intense enemy mortar and small arms fire. Passing through the ambush zone, First Lieutenant Wilson, with complete disregard for his own safety turned around and reentered the kill zone to insure the safe passage of the rear element of the convoy. While making this final courageous effort to insure the survival of his personnel, he was mortally wounded by an enemy mortar round falling on his vehicle. Through his extraordinary heroism and outstanding leadership ability, First Lieutenant Wilson was able to save the lives of many of his personnel who otherwise would have been halted in the kill zone subject to the most intense enemy fire. First Lieutenant Wilson's personal bravery and devotion to duty were in keeping with the highest traditions of the military service and reflects great credit upon himself, his unit, and the United States Army.

On December 8, 1968, the Bien Ho Cantonment Area, 124th Transportation Battalion (Truck) at Pleiku, Vietnam, was officially dedicated as "Camp Wilson" in memory of 1st LT David R. Wilson who was killed in action on January 31, 1968. A memorial plaque at Camp Wilson honors his memory. David was cited for his outstanding leadership and heroism in saving the lives of many of his men and was awarded the Silver Star Medal and the Purple Heart posthumously. The principal speaker at the ceremonies was Brig. General D. A. Richards, commanding general of all transportation units in II Corps, he told the assembled troops that 1st LT Wilson represented what they all were striving for:

> David Wilson knew the meaning of valor...the meaning of caring...the meaning of responsibility, and to me, David Wilson represents the hope for the future.

In another event to honor 1st LT Dave Wilson's bravery and heroism, there was a ceremony at an Armed Forces Reserve Center dedicated in his honor in Orlando, Florida, on October 4, 2003. The naming of this Center in Dave's honor was the result of the efforts and hard work of Colonel Dale Sindt, then in the US Army Reserve, who served with Dave Wilson as a platoon leader in Vietnam. David was known as a superior leader who possessed great personal bravery and unwavering devotion to duty. The Center covers 120,000 square feet and is a beautiful $16 million assembly hall, auditorium, and training facility. The following pictures are of the ceremony, the plaque, and the facility.

DEDICATED TO THE MEMORY OF
FIRST LIEUTENANT DAVID R. WILSON
64TH TRANSPORTATION COMPANY (MT)
BORN IN PITTSBURGH, PENNSYLVANIA 18 APRIL 1944
KILLED IN ACTION 31 JANUARY 1968
AWARDED THE SILVER STAR MEDAL
(POSTHUMOUS)
THIS ARMED FORCES RESERVE CENTER IS DEDICATED
AS A MEMORIAL TO HIS VALOR

64TH TC SILVER STAR

Front view as seen from
Armed Forces Reserve Drive

Rear view as seen from
Rear parking lot

USA
1LT. David R. Wilson
Armed Forces
Reserve Center
9500 Armed Forces
Reserve Drive
Orlando, FL 32827

<u>Facility Commander</u>

MG William S. Crupe

<u>Facility Manager</u>

Mr. Raymond Lopez

David Ralph Wilson

First Lieutenant

64TH TRANS CO, 124TH TRANS BN, 8TH TRANS GROUP, ARMY SPT CMD QUI NHON, 1ST LOG CMD, USARV

Army of the United States

Oreland, Pennsylvania

April 18, 1944 to January 31, 1968

DAVID R WILSON is on the Wall at Panel 36E, Line 43

See the full profile or name rubbing for David Wilson

14 Sep 2005

May you and the other Springfield High School personnel including my classmate Ricky Brooks rest in eternal peace. You will not be forgotten as long as one Vietnam Veteran survives.

Elmer M. Pence

THE VIRTUAL WALL ® VIETNAM VETERANS MEMORIAL www.VIRTUALWALL.org

Contact Us © Copyright 1997-2019 www.VirtualWall.org, Ltd ®(TM) Last update 08/15/2019

2/23/23, 2:43 PM www.VirtualWall.org Profile

David Ralph Wilson

ON THE WALL: **Panel 36E Line 43**

This page Copyright© 1997-2018 www.VirtualWall.org Ltd.

PERSONAL DATA:

Home of Record:	Oreland, PA
Date of birth:	04/18/1944

MILITARY DATA:

Service Branch:	Army of the United States
Grade at loss:	O2
Rank:	First Lieutenant
Promotion Note:	None
ID No:	05236011
MOS:	2136: Nontactical Unit Officer
Length Service:	01
Unit:	64TH TRANS CO, 124TH TRANS BN, 8TH TRANS GROUP, ARMY SPT CMD QUI NHON, 1ST LOG CMD, USARV

CASUALTY DATA:

Start Tour:	08/14/1967
Incident Date:	01/31/1968
Casualty Date:	01/31/1968
Status Date:	Not Applicable
Status Change:	Not Applicable
Age at Loss:	23
Location:	Binh Dinh Province, South Vietnam
Remains:	Body recovered
Repatriated:	Not Applicable
Identified:	02/10/1968
Casualty Type:	Hostile, died while missing
Casualty Reason:	Ground casualty
Casualty Detail:	Artillery, rocket, or mortar

URL: https://VirtualWall.org/dw/WilsonDR01a.htm

Data accessed: 2/23/2023

THE VIRTUAL WALL ® www.VirtualWall.org

Print This Page Close This Page

Page template 10/09/2015

Dave was only 23 years old when he lost his life, so young with an entire life ahead of him. It was a tragic loss of a young man with such a bright future. RIP...fellow Cadet, Vietnam Veteran and TKE Brother...YITB.

CHAPTER 10: FINAL THOUGHTS – HONOR & PMC LEGACY

HONOR

In the past year, I've learned a lot about these eight men and their strong families. Additionally, I have spoken with many other Vietnam Veterans whose war experiences have left me in awe. There have been many articles and books written about the Vietnam War, the difficult times here in the United States, and how the war impacted the country. This book has attempted to highlight the lives of eight brave men, Cadets from Pennsylvania Military College. It makes me wonder...of the 58,281 names on The Wall, how many of their stories have been told? Probably a few, but not enough I bet.

The men and women who served in Vietnam deserve every praise and plaudit for their service that they earned but never received! For these eight young men and their families, I hope this book honors their bravery, heroism and their ultimate sacrifices for this great nation.

HONOR

What is Honor?

A veteran - whether active duty, retired, National Guard or Reserve - is someone who, at one point in their life, wrote a blank check made payable to The United States of America for an amount "up to and including my life."

That is HONOR and there are way too many people in this country who no longer understand it.

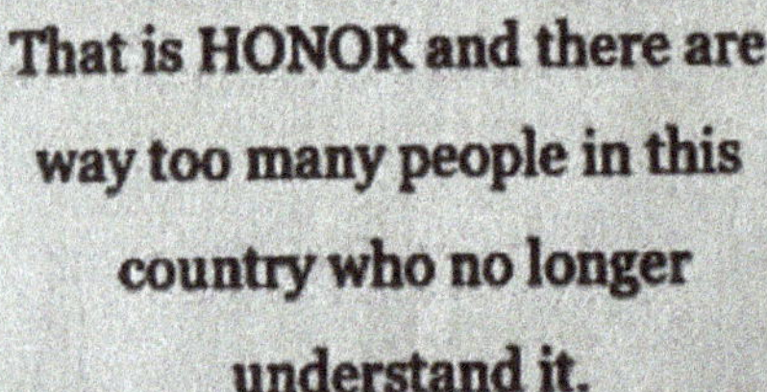

--Author Unknown

PMC LEGACY

It all started in 1821 and ended in 1972, one hundred and fifty one years of a military tradition of training boys in the ways of life in the military and turning them into men and true leaders. Traditions of uniforms, parades, respect, and love of God and Country, honor and service to our country no matter what war or conflict or foreign soil, PMC Alumni served with honor, bravery, dignity, and pride and represented their Alma Mater with distinction. Some, as we discussed in this book, made the ultimate sacrifice for this great nation.

In 1972, the Pennsylvania Military College colors were retired for good...a sad day for many of us. The Vietnam War had not only taken its toll on the lives of 58,281 men and women, but it also claimed the life of the second oldest military school in the nation. PMC is now Widener University. It sits on the same campus where the Cadets used to live, and utilizes some of the same dorms and facilities, but a lot has changed. There are new buildings; the campus has expanded. It is coed and has an ROTC unit called Company A of the Dauntless Battalion.

Life as a PMC Cadet was 24/7 in uniform during the academic year, with emphasis on military training, inspections, being a leader, marching and drilling, practicing maneuvers in local parks, and physical training.

Talking to my classmates while gathering research for this book and attending different PMC events at Widener, I felt a sense of extreme pride in having attended and graduated from Pennsylvania Military College. The graduates know their training at PMC provided a solid foundation for a career in the military or in their civilian life if they left the service when their commitment was complete. I was in the Class of 1968 and I still hear this comment today...55 years later...that's impressive! PMC Alumni are a select group of men who belong to an exclusive "fraternity" whose membership was closed in 1972. As a friend of mine says:

"Once a PMC Cadet, always a PMC Cadet!"

To date, there have been different approaches being studied by some PMC Alumni to enhance the PMC Legacy so the 151 years of PMC's history is not forgotten, and I applaud their efforts. This group of PMC alumni has formed a Legacy Committee. Most of us understand that PMC is no more; we know Widener is the future...as it should be. If we, the alumni of PMC, wish to have an honored and memorable legacy, then the current training of future officers in the armed forces of our nation through Company A at Widener needs to be supported. The word "legacy" is difficult to define especially considering the considerable emotions involved. I understand. But PMC was completely different from the Widener of today and sometimes the PMC Alumni have a difficult time embracing the reality.

How can the PMC Alumni be involved in the Legacy Committee, A Continuum of Excellence whose objectives are supporting future members of Widener University and Company A of the Dauntless Battalion? How can we foster the PMC legacy? I have spoken to Jim Love, a classmate, and Chuck Cantley, Class of '69, both members of the Committee, and asked for updates on their progress. Initial plans such as establishing a scholarship, financial assistance for incoming freshmen/women into the ROTC Program, the possibility of awards, etc., are all being considered. Other items are being discussed as well. The Committee is trying to get as many PMC Alumni involved either through donations and/or more activity with the current Widener administration and ROTC Staff. As I write this in April of 2023, a new Widener president has been installed. Her name is Dr. Stacey Robertson. Initial impressions indicate her support of the PMC Legacy. The three pillars of her administration are Recruiting, Retention, and Belonging.

As Chuck Cantley has stated to me: "The committee's objective is to work with key members of the Administration in helping design ways to enhance recruiting for the ROTC Program, thus enhancing the enrollment for Widener University as a whole. This is evident in the Purpose Statement [see next page] that the committee established as a guiding principle."

Chuck also commented: "The Legacy Committee encourages PMC Alumni to offer ideas and provide support as they are able. Dr. Stacey Robertson, the new President of Widener University was briefed on the Legacy Committee and stated, 'This is a win-win for everyone.'" Chuck believes the Committee has her support.

PURPOSE STATEMENT

TO: Perpetuate and enhance the Pennsylvania Military College-Widener legacy by utilizing the 150 years of values that Pennsylvania Military College (PMC) embraced in academics, integrity, leadership, military education and training and other qualities that distinguish Widener from other colleges and universities.

IN A WAY THAT:

- Recognizes Widener University as a premier academic leader and development institution by highlighting contributions to America from PMC Alumni,
- Emphasizes the contributions and commitments of PMC Cadet alumni and Widener Alumni to America through presentations of distinguished leaders and others at historical events,
- Broadens the recognition of the historical importance of PMC,
- Partners in developing an encompassing marketing plan to recruit and retain highly qualified students, highlighting leadership development,
- Increases student Reserve Officer Training Corps (ROTC) enrollment and retention by demonstrating the lineage of the PMC legacy and highlighting leadership development,

SO THAT: Over the next few years there is a definitive increase in the student population, a recognition that Widener is the place to be, an ROTC Program offering in depth leadership training that results in an overall increase to Widener's ranking and recognition, and the history and contributions of those associated with Pennsylvania Military College are not forgotten.

I couldn't think of a better way to end this book than reading the following article written by renowned columnist Ed Gebhart from the *Delaware County Daily Times* on April 1, 1994. Ed sums up his feelings about PMC, The Corps, and Jack Geoghegan. Well said Mr. Gebhart and thank you!

To all the PMC Graduates who over the years answered their country's call to serve in every war and conflict in which the United States has been engaged, thank you for your service. The PMC Legacy continues.

47 DELAWARE COUNTY DAILY TIMES Friday, April 1, 1994 47

OPINION & COMMENTARY

PMC's Corps of Cadets

By

ED GEBHART

I must confess to a lifelong love-hate relationship with the Corps of Cadets at what once was Pennsylvania Military College. The school is named Widener University now, but to anyone growing up in this area it probably always will be "PMC."

The "hate" business (that's probably too strong a word; "intense dislike" would be more like it) begun during my teen years when getting a date with a good looking girl was more important than breathing.

It was tough enough competing with my Chester High classmates and those love-starved clowns from St. James for a comely female's favors. But when the Cadets from PMC entered the competition, we home-boys seldom stood a chance.

The Cadets had those fancy uniforms, of course, and you knew they came from money or they wouldn't be attending PMC in the first place. Worse yet, they seemed to zero in on all the good looking girls in the First Ward, a territory I had staked out as my very own.

You finish runner-up to some rich, educated, good-looking dude from New York enough times, it's enough to give you a complex.

It wasn't until much later that my feelings about the institution changed. I hadn't know that one of the greatest men I even met, the late Francis "Bean" Brennan, had been a PMC Cadet. Later, I heard the stories of the McCaffery brothers during World War II and Col. Walt Layer during the Korean War.

And when local boys I knew as regular guys — like Jack Klotz, John Udovich, Jody Ambrosino and Eddie Walsh — became Cadets, I decided PMC wasn't such a bad place afterall.

Over the years, I met a lot of those "rich, good looking dudes" from New York and New Jersey and decided they weren't so bad either...fellows like Duke Crate and John DiShaw and Jack Martins and Joe Carter.

One of the fellows I never got to meet was a lad named John Lance Geoghegan — "Lance" to his doting parents in upstate New York, just plain "Jack" at PMC where he served as the highest ranking Cadet in the Corps and class president two years in a row.

He was in the Class of 1963 along with Delco kids like Allen Brewster, Albie Filoreto, Larry O'Hara, Joe Giampalmi, George Burke, Nick Trainer and George Stratts. Dave McNulty, now a Springfield attorney, also was in that class; and I'm indebted to him for bringing Geoghegan's story to light.

Geoghegan was one of those green lieutenants sent to lead our equally green troops in Vietnam during the early days of that conflict. He hardly fit the description of the red-eyed killers and child-murderers the Peace Movement (read draft dodgers) made our boys out to be.

On the contrary, Jack even postponed his commission for two years so he and his young bride, Barbara, could serve two years in Tanzania, Africa, with the Catholic Relief Services.

It was Geoghegan's fate to be right in the middle of one of the most memorable battles of the entire Vietnam experience. It was fought in a place called Ia Drang and pitted a First Cavalry Division battalion of 457 officers and men against two regiments of North Vietnamese regulars, totaling about 3,000. The odds were 8-to-1 against.

Before it was over, the battalion would lose 79 dead and 121 wounded. The enemy lost an estimated 1,300 dead. Both sides declared a victory.

Geoghegan commanded the second platoon of Charlie Company, the outfit that took the brunt of the Vietcong attack. On the second day of the three-day battle, the handsome, red-haired officer was in a two-man foxhole, firing away, when he heard one of his men, 24-year-old Willie Godboldt of Florida, yell for help.

A sergeant in the foxhole with Geoghegan said he would go to Willie's aid, "No," Geoghegan ordered, "I will."

As he moved out of the foxhole, young Jack Geoghegan — five days past his 24th birthday, father of six-month-old Camille — was shot through the back and head and was killed instantly.

The names of Lt. John Lance Geoghegan and PFC Willie F. Godboldt are next to each other on "The Wall."

Weeks later, when Geoghegan's grieving widow received his personal effects, she read the last letter he had written.

"I had a chance to go on R and R, but my men are going into action," he wrote. "I cannot and will not leave them now."

That's the story of Jack Geoghegan, one of nine PMC men to die during the Vietnam War.

I think about men like John Lance Geoghegan whenever I see that old World War II movie, "Midway," about the great naval battle that turned the tide in that war.

There is a scene where the immortal U.S. Navy "Torpedo Eight" squadron flies defiantly into a wall of withering fire and certain death to try to sink a Japanese aircraft carrier.

On the carrier, a Japanese admiral surveys their valor with awe and exclaims, "Where do they find such men?"

Part of the answer, Admiral, would be, "At Pennsylvania Military College."

Ed Gebhart is a public relations executive for a major corporation. His column appears Friday.

PENNSYLVANIA MILITARY COLLEGE ALUMNI WHO DIED IN SERVICE TO THE NATION

Civil War

Peach Ridgway Taliaferro
Zadoc Aydelotte
Alfred E. Townsend
Samuel H. Bolton
Henry Clay Robinett

Philippine-American War

John A. Logan, Jr.

WWI

Edmund Garretson Cook
David G. Allen
Bernard J. Cahn
Phelps R. Holman
Elliot Durand
Parker Vanamee
Joseph C. Morris Small
Douglas Tilford Cameron
Henry DeHority
John Irving Burns
George B. Murtha

WWII

Hugh F. McCaffery
Charles H. Terry
William Franklin Spang
Clarence E. Myers
S. Ellsworth Duff
Gordon M. Bettles
Daniel A. London
Joseph P. McCaffery
James G. Lynch
Herbert R. Amey, Jr.
Benjamin Ralph Kimlau
Jack Shoyer
Thomas R. O'Malley
Richard O'Malley
Walter Joseph Czarnecki
Robert Francis Spleen
Robert S. Currier
Roscoe N. D. Gray
Herbert Bailey
Peter E. Buck II
Milton R. Matteson, Jr.
Adam John Bassetti
Frank H. McCracken
Russell A. Freas, Jr.
William A. Cortwright
John Charles Williams III
Marshall V. Moss
William H. Derr
John Howard Faust
William R. Maddock Jr.
William T. Gardner

George Wilkens
Samuel H. Rosenbaum
William F. Callahan Jr.
William J. Wolfgram
Michael Richard Pessolano
James W. Gilbert, Jr.
James L. Flood
Edward Gazarian

Korean War

David W. Shute
Emery M. Hickman
Donald Elsworth Olmstead
Alan Stiteler
Frank Montagnolo

Vietnam War

John Lance Geoghegan
William J. Stephenson
Daniel F. Monahan
David R. Wilson
Dennis R. P. Isom
William J. Ahlum
Robert N. Chinquina
Robert H. Aldrich

Printed in the USA
CPSIA information can be obtained
at www.ICGtesting.com
LVHW010108060424
776610LV00001B/12